Dedicated to Peter and
our grandchildren, the future.

A J Hull, nee Elkington, was born in India to an army family, and spent most of her early childhood abroad.

She moved to North Norfolk in 1968 with her future husband and made it her home, raising her four children here.

She went to the Royal School, Bath and was awarded a degree in Psychology from UCL in 1965 and an MPhil in consultation in local government from UEA in 2000.

Her life in Norfolk was mostly spent as a mother, grandmother, teacher and a campaigner for peace, the environment and social justice.

For many years she was a single parent. But for the last 16 she has been living with her partner Peter.

She published a book on Kindle a few years ago. It is a political fable, 'The Roar of the Wind through the Trees'

CONTENTS

Foreword

I started this book many years ago, when the dangerous direction of travel in British politics was obvious to me. I was spurred on by the elephants in the room, many important topics being ignored, and the obvious fallacies being accepted. Too often the accepted view was the opposite of what was really happening. Since then Austerity, Brexit, the climate and ecological disasters, the increasingly disastrous social conditions in Britain, and global wars, migration and starvation, have all confirmed my fears and made the task more urgent but also much more difficult as situations have changed so rapidly. The information is overwhelming.

Very lately Covid19 has introduced major changes. Most of this book was written without considering the threat of pandemics. I was as unconcerned about this as many others. However, I find it entirely credible that pandemics are another result of the destruction of natural systems that our policies have caused. That pandemics will occur more frequently because people have become too close to wild life and its viruses as we have impinged on their habitats. I also find it credible that intensively farmed birds or animals have compromised immune systems and are therefore more vulnerable to new viruses. And that only one small change in the virus is needed for the people who tend them to get infected; hence avian flu and swine flu.

Having accepted that climate change, species extinction and coronaviruses are different aspects of the same problem, everything learned from Covid19 has proved highly relevant. Indeed, during lockdown I have learnt so much about the threats facing us, the incompetence of government and the possible solutions offered by thousands of individuals, communities and institutions that it has been difficult to finish this book. Every day brings vital new information.

3

Before looking for solutions, this book attempts to address the reasons behind the appalling state our systems of government and policies have brought us to. To the best of my knowledge, the combination of capitalism, military power, rapid technological change, and the interaction between communities with different faiths, ethos and political and legal systems that comes from globalisation, has produced a perfect storm of disasters which threatens civilisation and even the survival of life on earth.

Clearly many problems are global, but the UK has played a particularly shameful role in encouraging destructive policies and we have particularly undemocratic practices, so I shall first look at our toxic system, its possible causes and their repercussions. Then, lastly at how to repair the damage at home and globally.

What do I have to offer? My early life probably gave me an outsider's view and a more global one. I was born in India to an English army family, where the unconditional love of my India Ayah, Theresa, was the formative influence in my first years. I still feel she made me who I am. Later in Germany with the occupying forces, our German housemaids and driver provided normal friendly company while my parents struggled to adapt to life together after 5 years of separation during which they had both changed.

I was lucky to have a father so unprejudiced that, along with other officers, he went back to testify to the decent behaviour of the Japanese commander of his POW camp. (In vain as it happens. The commander was shot.) And we brought Irmgarde, one of our German maids, back to England with us. From her I learned how impossible it was to stand against the Nazis once they were in power. Her brother was in the SAS against his wish. Once invited he was unable to refuse as his family would have paid the price.

Later, as an 'unimportant' adult I have not suffered the pressures on those in the heat of action. This has given me the time to listen and think about things more slowly.

I have learnt a great deal by joining national campaigns, and one campaign has often led to others. My first cause was against nuclear weapons. Coming from an army family in the 40s, war was constantly on my mind. The minute I heard about nuclear weapons I knew they were terribly wrong. How could a weapon of mass destruction be used for defence? I have campaigned against nuclear weapons since the first Aldermaston marches, volunteering in the London office in the 60s, and running Holt for Peace with some friends in the 80s when Angie Zelter, the famous environmental campaigner, taught me a lot. As a result, I took part in her Snowball Campaign in the 80's, cutting a strand of wire at the Sculthorpe airbase to argue our case in court. And much later in 2015 I collected signatures for PICAT – the Public Interest Court Action Against Trident in 2015.

A two year part time Cambridge Extra Mural course on the nuclear arms race added greatly to my knowledge. This was offered to the Holt Peace group by Dr Gwyn Prins after he gave a talk about the nuclear Freeze campaign. I became the local organiser. In the end his teaching lasted for 4 years, the last 2 being on North-South issues. There were also visits from several other speakers. We occasionally went to Cambridge. I transcribed a series of talks recorded as Volume 2 in 'Nuclear Dilemmas' for Cambridge Extra Mural Courses. When the Berlin Wall came down many of us went to a series of talks recorded and published as 'Spring in Winter'.

I am very grateful to this course. It not only enlarged the knowledge I had from a degree in Psychology and Social Anthropology, it also changed my attitude. It gave me the confidence to trust my gut feelings. Ever since teenage times, while unable to give up my heartfelt convictions, I had feared that they were not practical. That hardnosed ideas were the realistic ones. The result was that I felt helpless to do anything useful – despite my campaigning habit. Most of the information on these courses confirmed my views. They demonstrated that my views, always dismissed as fanciful ideals by my family, had been accurate and practical. That gut feelings are important and should be taken seriously. It led me to realise that ideals, such as the ten commandments or treating your neighbour like yourself are in fact practical recipes for harmonious living - the very opposite of 'fanciful ideas'. Critically the courses also taught me the importance of facing up to dilemmas, researching situations in detail and picking apart statements to test if they are true or false.

Campaigning on roads followed. I had had a small personal success which may have encouraged me. Highways were planning to demolish two pretty cottages on a bend at the entrance of my village to straighten the road. When one cottage became empty, Highways were only waiting for the other to follow before demolishing both. My canvass of the village showed support for both the cottage and the bend, so a friend managed to rent the empty cottage. And while she was there, taking advice from a local solicitor, we had the cottage spot listed from London.

This was my first encounter with local politics. Had we not used London the local Highways team would have demolished the cottage before it could be listed. A useful lesson. The Council did not forgive us. When a few years later a builder restored the cottage he was harried and delayed all the way. Then, to complete the irony, the Council congratulated itself by giving the cottage a conservation award.

Another apparent local success, achieved by three of us, was the cancellation of the proposed Letheringsett bypass across some water meadows. (although I think cost was probably the real reason for this U-turn.) I was prompted into this by my children who declared this was the worst thing that had happened. They loved the water meadows. I thought it just meant a couple of letters – but the campaign took years, and taught me more about local politics and the vitriolic emotions they raise.

This campaign changed my life in two ways. It brought me to the attention of the Green Party which I joined and later worked with locally. It also led to several years part time research on the Consultation in two road schemes at Norfolk County Council Highways, completed as an MPhil in 2000. At the time I was asking several organisations if they knew of any way I could help 'green' our way of life by working part time from home. This was my only offer. I don't think it changed anything, but it certainly taught me a lot about the inadequacies of local councils; the fiction of consultation, the crass systems used to assess benefits and costs, and the poverty of ideas in both officers and councillors.

Sadly, nearly all my campaigning with others both on roads, nuclear weapons or other topics seems to have been fruitless. Campaigning against Trident in Holt High Street saw a big change in public opinion. At first it was only a few 'hippies' who signed our petitions. Most people avoided eye contact, or crossed the road to avoid us. But after a few years, many more signed and every sort of person crossed the road to talk to us. But government policy remained the same. Similarly, the campaign against the Norwich Ring Road made no impact on the County Council. Indeed, they managed to 'lose' the objections.

Learning about other topics came from my involvement with the local Environmental Forum in the 90s – a response to the UN Rio Environmental Summit of 1992. I was specifically involved in two local projects - to improve recycling and to provide a community wind turbine. In both cases the District Council let us down. They were happy for us to do lots of work but didn't take us seriously. With recycling, we were encouraged to carry out 2 pilot studies to test if people would collect items separately at home, when the Council had already agreed a different contract.

Regarding the community turbine – it finally got to planning after 7 year's work by volunteers including myself, raising grants and local investments to carry out all the expensive pre planning surveys required. However, not one councillor stood up to put the record straight when aggressive anti wind campaigners flooded the area with grossly misleading leaflets. This despite the fact that the councillors had supported the project at the start and had been kept in touch with developments all along. Two sad lessons about local politics.

The local District Council remained implacably against onshore wind, They claimed to speak for the public, as they were supported by one vociferous local group. But of course they ignored the obvious support for onshore wind from the many who had invested in the proposal at North Walsham. The Council spent taxpayers' money on going to court over two local smallish wind turbines proposed by farmers, which were supported by the independent inspectors. Even after the council had declared a climate emergency, they expressed 'regret' that they could not fight the turbines a third time, and imposed a very tight timetable on the developers.

I first heard of GMOs when a member of the forum. I felt the same instant dread of GMOs as I had of nuclear weapons. Both spoke of the arrogance of mankind, interfering with things beyond their control. Through the Forum I organised and transcribed three memorable talks during the national consultation on GMOs. In 2003. Since then I have been kept informed by the GM Freeze and subsequent campaigns.

It is clear that most of my learning has come from other peoples' work - whistle blowers in campaigning groups, such as CND, GM Freeze, Greenpeace, Oxfam, CAAT, Eradicating Ecocide, etc and from many books. The Guardian has been a constant source of information over the last decades, and, with my poor memory and grasp of detail, Wikipedia has proved invaluable for checking facts.

There's nothing new in most of my ideas. They have been and are being expressed better by others. I hope that pulling together a range of simple facts and revealing false myths at a time when trust in government has been severely undermined by their failure to protect us from Covid19, will make people more open to the truth. They will understand the urgency of the environmental crises, their link to the social disasters of the age and possible solutions. It's not as though countless warnings have not been given. Thousands of people have been and still are urging for sustainable change for the planet and its peoples. The information is there even if not in government statements or the main media.

I hope the suggestions made will chime with the wishes of ordinary people, the majority, who care most for their families and friends and are not dominated by the love of money and power which infects our leaders. And who have learnt through lockdown something about their own power to communicate and work with others.

Lastly, I hope this book may be an anti-dote to conspiracy theories, although the book has exposed several actions that can only be described as conspiracies. Mistaken beliefs and prejudices underlie many mistakes. They becomes conspiracies when the mistake is obvious and yet a group of people pursue the same policy because it is to their own selfish advantage. And they deliberately mislead others into compliance. Austerity is a classic case.

The world is clearly full of conspiracies, both criminal and political but conspiracy theories don't help. My impression is that they soon get out of hand and increasingly fanciful. But their worst handicap in dealing with democracies is that they take no account of the public. The impression is of an all powerful elite totally in control. A hopeless situation and an unrealistic one. The public are not helpless. A government can only rule with their compliance. Once many more people understand the false myths of government as well as the damaging class and racist prejudices which have divided them, they can come together to build a safer world. As ever, democracies depend on the knowledge and intelligence of the public. We fall or survive according to our abilities.

Why an ABC? Partly because the topic is so big I had to research it that way, going slowly through topics, such as, in 'A': Austerity, Air pollution, Allies, Afghanistan, Affluenza; in 'B'; Banks, Benefits, Bonuses, etc. Partly to acknowledge it can only be, at best, a very simple book, a beginner's book, a first reader. My task has been, like the little boy in the Hans Anderson story, to show that the emperor has no clothes and to offer simple potential solutions. Other more informed people will need to add vital information, facts, figures and ideas.

Acknowledgements

The sources other than my own experience and studies which have largely been books, campaign material, TV programmes, videos and talks, have been loosely arranged into categories for simplicity.

The information about the growing environmental crises, apart from news items and UN reports, came from several campaigning groups, Greenpeace and their recent weekly updates 'Unearthed', Friends of the Earth (FOE), Butterfly Conservation and Wildlife groups and more recently Extinction Rebellion; Also from James Lovelock's seminal book 'Gaia: A New Look at Life on Earth.' Simon Reeves programmes also give many snapshots of environmental destruction and social inequality and distress, but also of the beauty of the world and the strength and humanity of people.

Information about the dangers of nuclear weapons, nuclear power and NATO came from CND campaign material, and two books, 'Protest and Survive' by E P Thompson and 'World in Chains', edited by Angie Zelter. Information about our increasingly hostile nuclear policy came from the British American Safety Information Council (BASIC).

Information about the arms industry, the horror it causes, its cost to tax payers and the corruption involved, came from the Campaign Against the Arms Trade (CAAT), and the book 'As Used on the Famous Nelson Mandela' by Mark Thomas. Information about the irrelevance of arms in combating today's threats came from 'Top Guns and Toxic Whales' by Gwyn Prins.

Information about our colonial past came from the books 'The Last Mughal' by William Dalrymple, and 'Inglorious Empire; What the British did in India' by Shash Tharoor, the former Under-Secretary General at the UN, and MP for the Congress Party in India. Also from programmes about slavery and its effects in Britain by Professor David Olusoga.

The linked information about the effect of recent global neo-colonial corporate exploitation comes from several campaigns over the years to cancel the debt; the video of a conversation between Russell Brand and Dr Jason Hickel, Anthropologist 'Inequality is Killing us. Are We Going to Stop it?', one in the series 'Under the Skin'; and talks by Vandana Shiva and two of her books, 'Biopiracy' and 'Who Really Feeds the World'. Regarding the all important topic of food, Felicity Lawrence in her books, such as 'Not on the Label' and her Guardian articles, adds information about the unhealthy food produced in the West and the lax regulations which allow adulteration and worse.

More information about the perfidy of western governments, and their inability to understand or deal with other cultures, comes from the video, 'The Accidental Anarchist' by Carne Ross, a former diplomat; the film 'Bitter Lake' by Adam Curtis and a TV series on the Vietnam War which gave testimonies from both sides; as well as the book 'Murder in Samarkand' by Craig Murray, Ambassador to Uzbekistan until he was removed from his post in October 2004.

Information about the scale and mechanisms used to impose undemocratic control in national and global institutions comes from the Corbett Report 'How and Why Big oil Conquered the World' as well as the information from Jason Hickel and Vandana Shiva, listed above.
Information about the dangers inequality poses even in richer countries comes from 'The Precariat: The New Dangerous Class' by Guy Standing, Professor of Development Studies at the London School of African and Oriental Studies.

The information about the character traits associated with greedy capitalist exploitation comes from 'The Selfish Capitalist: Origins of Affluenza' by Oliver James, a psychologist who has learnt much from treating the unhappy rich.

Information about a range of solutions to both the environmental and social crises also came from many of those already listed, including Guy Standing, Jason Hickel and Vandana Shiva. In addition, from many campaign groups trying to build back better including 'Black Lives Matter', Local Futures and contributors to Compass zoom meetings and Green Party events. Also critically the books: 'Drawdown – The Most Comprehensive Plan Ever Proposed to Reverse Global Warming', edited by Paul Hawken; 'Wilding' by Isabella Tree, 'Climate Justice - Hope, Resilience and the Fight for a Sustainable Future' by Mary Robinson, former President of Ireland and UN Special Envoy on Climate Change, 'Doughnut Economics' by Kate Raworth, 'No One Is Too Small To Make a Difference' by Greta Thunberg and 'Small is Beautiful' by E F Schumacher as well as the report by Professor Catherine Rowett 'Energising the East'.

I must express my gratitude to all the varied the campaigners, whistle blowers, who have kept the public informed over the years. In no particular order they include Greenpeace, Friends of the Earth, GM Freeze, The Soil Association, CPRE, RSPB, Amnesty, Occupy, Shelter, CND, CAAT, Jubilee Debt Campaign, War on Want, World Development Movement, Transport 2000, OXFAM, Eradicating Ecocide, Black Lives Matter, Hope not Hate, Stop the War, Build Back Better, Possible, AVAAZ, SumOfUs, Freedom United, Local Futures, Extinction Rebellion, FridaysforFree, Change.org, 38 degrees, and the Green Think Tank. Also to my friends and family who have prompted me to watch programmes, and read books and have even given me some.

Chapter 1   Democracy

I start from the simple view taught me at school, that democracy, the rule 'of the people, by the people, for the people' is the safest form of government in contrast to hereditary rulers, war lords, dictators or one-party states.   This view seems to fit with the evidence of history. Centuries of brutal and uncaring treatment of large sections of the population resulted from the whims, beliefs and interests of powerful rulers.   They cannot be relied on to be benign. We all know that individuals can go mad, that power frequently corrupts and that rulers get out of touch and so are ignorant as well as uncaring about the living conditions of the public.

Democracy does not imply fewer mistakes.   We all make mistakes. Democracy is only safer because those in power can be voted out if their ideas fail badly enough, in contrast to tyrants who can hang on to self-serving power for decades.

Democracy clearly implies that our own rulers are often a threat, maybe one of the greatest threats, to our wellbeing.

Democracy has inevitable weaknesses.   Democratic control tends to apply only to the country itself.   It makes sense for people to react to their own living conditions for entirely selfish reasons, but they would need to be considerably more enlightened to care for those of others. A country's policies overseas can have disastrous results and be seriously destabilising, but still not become part of political choices at home.   International rules agreed between countries are needed for fairness.   These have become all too important in today's global world. Another weakness is short term thinking, although this may well apply to all systems.

In general, we are bad at thinking ahead.   In a democracy, those in power will be tempted to keep in power by making promises to please in the very near future. They will be less likely to undertake tasks, particularly costly ones, for the long term, which may mean pain now and when any advantage may not be recognised as their work. It may not enhance their reputation.

The contradictory roles for MPS in representative democracy are a particular strain. MPs are expected both to represent, which requires listening, and to lead, which implies being able to push through their own views. In a well functioning democracy, MPs will be well informed about the outcomes of policies and act accordingly, even when not popular. They are expected to know more than the public and to do their very best to explain their views. Classic example are the repeal of capital punishment which was almost certainly out of step with popular opinion and the imposition of seat belts. Both successful civilising decisions.

The other side of the equation also has its dangers. It is very easy for voters to leave everything to the government under the tempting illusion that 'they know best'. A lazy electorate is not healthy. MPs make mistakes. They need to be criticised and held to account by an intelligent and active public.

Over the last decades, successive parliaments have failed to lead on the gravest threats to our survival – nuclear weapons and climate change, to which we must now add, species extinction, pandemics, economic disaster and inequality.

MPs over the decades have failed to examine the evidence, although it is their duty to know the dangers. As a result, there has been no real debate in Parliament about nuclear weapons – now Trident - only repetition of the same unproven simplistic platitudes. And gross complacency and creative accounting about policies to combat climate breakdown. It is clear that our representative democracy is not functioning properly.

Democracy is clearly vulnerable. The rise of Hitler by the use of democratic procedures showed us that. In Germany's case, the combination of deep public distress from an impossible economic situation and a skilled orator prepared to use any trick or lies to divide the nation to fit his perverted aims, was enough to overcome democratic rule. We should learn from that sad experience about the social conditions and the sort of leadership which threaten democracy.

Democracy can only function under certain conditions, free speech, a fair voting system and an independent judiciary. I believe that our system has failed and continues to fail because it lacks some of these essential conditions.

Chapter 2 – Conditions necessary for democracy; fair representation

The most basic need for a democratic system is a fair system of representation. In the UK we have almost universal suffrage, although some would wish 16 and 17 year olds be included. But our voting system has been broken for decades. The first-past-the-post system can only work when there are just two parties. For decades it has guaranteed unrepresentative government. It has allowed one of the two main parties to gain a majority in government, and impose its policies, when only representing a minority of the population.

The figures make it clear. For example, in 2015, the Tory party gained a small majority in Parliament with only 36.9% of the vote, from a turnout of only 66.4%. This means that David Cameron held the referendum with the support of under 26% of the population.

The percentage of people not voting in the last few decades, about a third of the electorate, indicates how unhappy many are with our voting system.

The system makes it incredibly difficult for new parties to get established. In 2015 the Green party had well over 1 million votes, but only one seat, as did UKIP with 3.88 million votes.

Critically, the voting system encourages the two major parties to restrict debate. They deliberately aim to deny alternative views 'the oxygen of publicity'. As a result, the population are denied information and ideas. Over decades this has undoubtedly led to a grossly uninformed public unable to hold MPs to account.

At election times, several factors lead to a vicious cycle. The BBC's rules ensure that smaller parties get less coverage. At the same time many people do not want to 'throw away' their vote. They want to vote for a party which has a chance of getting in. This leads to tactical voting, where the least awful party is chosen rather than one that is actually supported. Parties use fear or even hatred of the other in campaigning while alternative ideas are ignored. The system encourages divisive tactics.

Our historic class system has added to the problem as it is cemented into party politics today. Class still permeates most aspects of life - language, schooling, job prospects, respect from others, etc. It is a two tier system rather than an egalitarian one. It accepts the exploitation of some by others. The influence of class was so strong in politics that even when the welfare state was set up, at a time of unprecedented social cohesion after the Second World War, private health care and private (so called public) schools were still allowed.

The class system dominates the attitudes of the two major parties to this day. The Tories see themselves as natural leaders, with the confidence and arrogance that encourages. This is irrespective of the actual success of their policies. They still consider themselves the party best able to protect the economy after the disastrous recession in the 80s and following the appalling effects of Austerity. The Labour party seems to suffer from an inferiority complex, unable to promote some policies or defend others for fear of being seen as weak on defence, or the economy or soft on crime.

Old class loyalties, unthinking tribal behaviour, old suspicions, mutual disrespect, fierce competition and even hatred pervert party politics. Critically, middle class Tories and working class Labour do not co-operate. For decades any policy suggested by one side has almost inevitably been derided by the other, however illogical. This would be funny if it were not so damaging.

Fear of the other, typical of tribal thinking, has been a major tool of electioneering, with exaggerated claims and vilification, such as persistent claims that Jeremy Corbyn is a communist and racist. The idea, common on the continent, that politicians are colleagues, respecting each other and collaborating despite competition and disagreements, is entirely missing in the UK. A tragedy in the present crises and a big factor in the total impasse of Brexit.

Equally damaging, party discipline demands that individual MPs lie about their own views in order to support the bias of their party. (As far back as the 1960s I noticed that the packages of policies each party chose often did not seem to belong together logically. Nor were the same packages used in other countries.) Our system encourages unquestioning obedience and lying.

The importance of this should not be underestimated. We all lie sometimes, and often feel a bit uncomfortable about it. When lying is and has been a central part of political life it must have had an effect on society in general. Social media is often blamed for an increase in lying, fake news, but I think it is endemic in our society because it comes right from the top and has done so for decades. A general carelessness about being accurate is even common in many formal documents which do not fit the particulars of a case. It has become acceptable despite the fact that habitual lying is the tool of criminals.

'Winner takes all', the lure of total power for one of the major parties for the next 5 years, has eliminated co-operation and consensus in government and encouraged false claims at election times. Anything to get that majority by hook or crook. As a result, contrary to earlier visions of democratic behaviour, minority views, even from substantial minorities, are not respected. The two Tory governments since the Referendum have felt able to ignore the wishes of the 48%. This is always accompanied by early promises to 'unite'.

Over the decades debate has largely been replaced by simplistic sound bites using all the expertise of the advertising profession to manipulate people's views, aided by constant repetition.

The first past the post voting system has almost certainly persisted because it unfairly favours the two major parties. I find it shocking that both our major parties knowingly support a corrupt system. Even now, the Labour Party supports the system. Attempts over the last decades to get proportional representation have been blocked by them as much as the Tories. How realistic their hope for power has become with the loss of Scottish support and the threatened new boundary changes is questionable.

This corrupt system has been and still is a major cause of anger and alienation in the country. When unpopular policies, particularly those contradicting earlier promises, such as the Tory promise to protect the NHS, are pushed through, widespread public anger and frustration are inevitable. In addition, when for decades people have been unable to vote for anyone they can support, true for the majority who live in safe seats, they can feel with good reason, that they have no stake in our society. Many stop voting and this in turn means their needs are not considered. Election promises are aimed at those who vote. It is no surprise that society has become increasingly unequal.

The voting system is also a major cause of incompetence. When only a small group with a shared ideology form policy, they are almost certainly unaware of many potential unintended consequences. 'The devil is in the detail' or more accurately 'the information is in the detail.' Being able to push through policies without heeding the warnings of others is a recipe for disaster – as shown by the results of the experimental austerity programme imposed against the advice of all the professions affected - doctors, lawyers, judges, social workers, teachers, the police and traditional economists.

First-past-the-post has ensured an uninformed public and allowed uncaring, incompetent, even criminally negligent, policies.   These enabled the disasters of 'austerity' and the referendum. In general it has allowed gross inequality in the country and countless social problems; humanitarian catastrophes and illegal wars abroad and threatens climate, ecological and nuclear catastrophes.

Our first-past-the-post voting system does not represent the public and is at the heart of our dysfunctional democracy.

Chapter 3   Conditions Essential for Democracy – free speech, a free press

Three other conditions are essential for democracy, freedom of speech, a free press and an independent judicial system. All three are critical because they enable an informed public to hold government to account. The wish for democratic accountability recognises that 'leaders' of all sorts may not be benign. Their interests may, at worst, be a major threat to the population as a whole.

Theoretically we have freedom of speech unlike some other countries. Speaking our minds does not expose us to danger. But to a large extent we remain helpless because no notice is taken of dissenting views.
Indeed protesters, trying to alert the public and government by democratic means to what they consider real dangers, are often treated as enemies of the state and monitored by the secret services.

One small example; in the 80s a conversation between myself and a friend in CND was taped by the security services. We only discovered this when we were cut off and John said my last few words kept repeating eerily on a loop tape. If two unimportant, powerless individuals, using legal, peaceful methods of protest are being taped, how many more thousands of people are suspect and at what cost to the taxpayer?

We cannot claim that our free speech has led to healthy debate. I hope it flourishes somewhere, but many adults I have known suffer from a general inability to discuss politics or religion or anything serious. Serious topics are embarrassing, even rude, a conversation killer. One reason for this maybe the way disagreement is stifled in our political parties, by the party whips and collective cabinet decisions. This certainly cannot have helped. Political correctness is another force stifling debate.

But far more important, we do not have a free press. The dominant right-wing press promotes the interests of large corporations. Since 2010, their output has been in line with a government dedicated to market forces and largely funded by big business.

The circulation figures for daily papers alone show a huge preponderance of papers supporting right wing parties in recent elections. Well over 4 million copies supporting the policies of Conservatives, and more recently, UKIP and the Brexit party. This contrasts with figures for more left wing papers; the Daily Mirror with 508,705 copies and the Guardian with 141,160 copies.

Many papers have supported right wing views for several decades. They have been and are owned by billionaires with substantial business interests in banking, property and general business as well as publishing and the media. So, a few press barons, with global interests and fixed ideological views control countless publications here and across the world. Rupert Murdoch being the typical current example.

Close links with the Conservative politicians have been and are the norm, going back for decades. Very recently, George Osborne with the Evening Standard, Boris Johnson with the Telegraph.

No one should doubt the power of the press to influence the political climate in the UK. Clearly a press overwhelmingly in support of right wing, monetarist views, prioritising business and banking interests, severely diminishes public debate. Other views are ignored or not given a fair hearing.

But it is far worse. For decades the gutter press has been deliberately misleading the public with sensational fabrications and gratuitously hostile language. They have fostered jingoism, racism, homophobia, anti-European feelings, fear of migrants and climate change denial. They have also set out to destroy individual lives by character assassination. The Sun's series of false stories about Elton John resulted in a total of 17 libel writs.

To give just three examples; as long ago as 1924, the Daily Mail's forged Zinoviev letter, implied that British Communists were planning violent revolution and was thought significant in the defeat of Ramsay Macdonald.

In 2015, the United Nations High Commission for Human Rights objected to the language used by Katie Hopkins to describe migrants as "cockroaches" and "feral humans" "spreading like the norovirus" in The Sun. In 2017 over 100 cross party MPs condemned the fascist language used In an article in August by Trevor Kavanagh referring to "The Muslim Problem".

Even the Telegraph, which used to be thought of as a sober paper, failed to correct Johnson's many blatant falsehoods. In contrast the Guardian, financed by the Scott Trust Limited, is usually respected and trusted for accuracy in the many investigations it pursues.

Some right wing papers notorious for misinformation, are also known for illegal hacking, corrupt payments and other financial misdoings.
All papers are to some extent influenced by business interests as they all use advertising to cover their costs. In the 80's a successful freelance journalist from JANE (Journalists Against Nuclear Extermination) told a meeting in Norfolk that after she covered one CND event, she was blacklisted by all papers except the Guardian. She assumed it was because of their investments in weaponry.

In theory the BBC could and should provide an anti-dote to the interests of the press barons. Funded by the public, largely trusted to be independent and fair, and with a mandate to 'hold government to account' and 'to educate' it could and should give voice to the full range of views, providing proper education for the public.

The BBC is often criticised for being left wing in its coverage, but in fact its news programmes for many years have largely failed to provide any objective criticism of right wing governments. Since 2010 the news has repeated day in day out the claims of government without question. The financial crash was consistently blamed on the Labour party. Trident is consistently described as an independent minimum deterrent which has kept the peace.

The views of the right-wing press are given credibility and more publicity by being repeated in the news. Excessive publicity given to UKIP before the Euro elections in 2014 legitimised their divisive language and failed to question the incoherence of their policies. Over time, repeated falsehoods are accepted as facts by a largely trusting public.

This has been accompanied by a blackout on the positive alternatives so badly needed when current policies are failing. This includes ideas from the Green Party, the only political party not supporting monetarist policies. Indeed, it has worked to create the false impression that the Green Party only cares about the environment, when in fact Greens have always insisted that social justice relies on a healthy environment. The two are inextricably linked.

Similarly, Jeremy Corbyn's socialist views have been either ignored of falsely characterised as Marxist. While his willingness to talk to all sides has been construed as agreeing with our enemies. Winston Churchill was lauded for saying 'jaw jaw is better than war war' but the same behaviour from Jeremy has him branded as a traitor.

Even in the climate emergency it's been business as usual for the BBC news. Despite daily information about the increasingly drastic effects of global warming, the BBC has continued to talk of 'growth' as good, falling sales as 'bad', and failed to publicise the carbon costs of any project, only the financial ones. They quoted the government's carbon neutral targets, without pointing out these exclude air and sea traffic. Following the same pattern, dramatic climate actions in London were largely ignored, even when outside the BBC building.

The same failure to hold government to account has continued through the Brexit turmoil despite the very obvious failure of policy. At the time of the 2019 election, the BBC echoed the Leave mantra that people want 'to get Brexit settled' so that other concerns can be tackled, without pointing out that leaving will not settle anything. It is bound to start another long process. They also claimed a general election would decide the issue, without pointing out that a general election cannot produce a representative answer.

The BBC news has used the requirement for 'balance' over decades to undermine information about two major threats to our survival, climate change and nuclear war. Climate change deniers have been given as much publicity, and therefore as much credibility, as the views of 99% of world scientists. Opposition to Trident has been ignored and the falsely reassuring slogans of the government repeated.

'Balance' in practice often means that one proposal is cancelled out immediately with contradictory slogans from the other side, leaving people no better informed and so largely able to keep to their existing prejudices. But 'balance' is sometimes ignored. The close vote in the referendum was not reflected in coverage. It was usually Leave voters who were asked for their opinions.

The style of the BBC, simplistic slogans and short sound bites, adds to the problem. The short time given to topics does not allow the detailed look that situations require. This style echoes the behaviour of the main parties who wish to suppress debate. It increases their impact.

The result is a narrowed right-wing agenda, grossly degraded debate, inaccurate claims and a largely ignorant and brainwashed public unable to question the myths which suit the elite: The worst possible situation when the status quo has so obviously failed to produce harmony in the UK or the world. And new ideas are urgently needed to face the major threats of our time. Ignorant people cannot choose MPs wisely.

I must make a distinction between the news and other BBC programmes. Some are excellent at highlighting problems accurately. But then the mismatch between alarming information and the lack of political will or interest to act, only serves to demoralise all who care. It induces a sense of helplessness. The BBC news has supported the status quo, monetarist and right-wing ideologies. It has resisted change. It has acted for the elite. It probably is part of the elite. It certainly is part of the problem.

Chapter 4   Conditions Essential for democracy – an independent judiciary.

The fourth essential feature of democracies is an independent judiciary, able to question parliament. Democracy is unique in choosing to decide issues by law and negotiation. The older, more primitive way of settling arguments and possession by conquest gave way to a wish for decisions to be fair, based on ethical arguments and protected by the law. The government itself is recognised as a potential threat to fair rule which needs to be kept in check by an independent judiciary.

Our justice system, as it relates to government, has not been a total failure, despite being expensive and so only open to people with enough money. It has shown its independence in some situations, taking the government to court over air quality, health and safety, human rights and, in the Gina Miller case, to defend the power of parliament against the government.

However, international law, on which civilised conduct between nations relies, has suffered much more. With regard to nuclear weapons, a major threat to our survival, successive governments have not kept to their promise to get rid of nuclear weapons and have thereby weakened the law. International law depends on individual countries upholding it voluntarily.

The situation got considerably worse under Mrs May. She reneged on our previous position by removing the International Court of Justice (ICJ) from ruling on cases about nuclear weapons or nuclear disarmament. This change made disarmament harder precisely when hundreds of non-nuclear countries had come together in the UN to ban nuclear weapons. We had also quietly changed from our policy of only using nuclear weapons in retaliation, second strike, to allowing first strike use, including against a state without them.

In 2018, the Attorney General, the political link between government and the justice system, refused to allow court action against Trident and so denied public debate about its dangers and illegality. It is hard not to conclude that this legal decision was controlled by his political attitude. Humanitarian law, both international and domestic, has been undermined. This covers the duty to protect civilians in war, to protect human rights including those of commonwealth citizens and to provide asylum.

Our attitudes to international policies seem to have been perverted by our historic 'success' in colonisation which gave us a delusional and racist sense of superiority. The attitude that we are better than others is still very common in the UK. Class divisions in the UK seem to have morphed in the colonies into institutional racism. People in or from other countries, even when legally British Citizens, were, and still are, cast in the role of the underdog and denied basic rights.

Racism and delusions of superiority have encouraged broken commitments in international and domestic humanitarian law, and contributed to the mistreatment of refugees, migrants. (And indeed, since the referendum, other Europeans.) Only the very wealthy are excepted.

We choose to ignore the inconvenient facts that the colonies were subjugated by force and exploited, their lands stolen, their culture misunderstood and undervalued, their social and political systems destroyed, and random boundaries imposed. All of which caused huge problems which continue to this day.

When studying Social Anthropology in the 60s I learnt that the missionaries in Africa who accompanied soldiers and business interests, did everything they could to destroy the particular native religious beliefs and rituals of each small scale society. These beliefs were an essential part of the social organisation of most indigenous societies. In the following predictable social collapse the missionaries accused their victims of being drunk and degenerate.

India provides the starkest example. A highly civilised and wealthy industrial power was completely destroyed by the ruthless, immoral and cruel behaviour of the East Indian Company and the British government. In 'Inglorious Empire' Shash Tharoor describes the countless ways by which Indian wealth was transferred to England. Indeed the blatant corporate greed of the East Indian Company is a terrifying early example of the corporate greed now typical of globalisation.

In more recent times, as we all now know, migrants from the colonies, who were invited here to help us, were treated badly. I lived in London in the 50s and 60s when the tube trains and hospitals relied on African and Caribbean workers, but accommodation signs said 'no Blacks, no Irish, no dogs'. Inevitably, ghettos developed with desperately overcrowded and poor accommodation, bringing its own problems. The gutter press lived up to their reputation, inciting racism and religious intolerance. Migrants, so easily identified by colour and dress, were perfect scapegoats.

In today's world, the number of refugees is increasing driven by climate change, poverty, war and persecution. It includes asylum seekers and those escaping poverty – economic migrants. The UK has continued to be hostile to all migrants except the very rich. Despite the facts that our disruptive colonial history, our involvement in global businesses and wars in the Middle East have been the root causes of migration. And that our wealth should enable us to contribute significantly, every effort has been made to stop people coming here. International humanitarian law is being continually undermined.

David Cameron, must bear significant responsibility for the unfolding tragedy of refugees' lives. When he turned down Angela Merkel's statesman like proposal that EU countries share migrants, he encouraged other countries to be equally hostile. This led eventually to the disastrous decision to use Turkey, a country on the edge of conflict, with a poor record on human rights. And must have contributed to the appalling distress in Greece and Italy.

Predictably, he used a series of callous arguments to portray migrants as tempted by traffickers to undertake dangerous journeys. The fact that they were being driven from their homes by bombs, persecution or starvation, were ignored. Under the cynical guise of saving lives, the problem became one of stopping the traffickers and turning back the boats, which continues to this day.

David Cameron was prepared to spend money for refugees to be kept in other countries, whatever tensions and pressures this caused – anywhere else as long it wasn't here. Mrs May used our geographic position to declare we should not be involved. Once here, traumatised refugees were treated abominably under Mrs May's hostile environment, and have continued to be so.

In the arguments for Brexit, migrants were the scapegoats, taking the blame for failed economic and housing policies. The Leave campaign, especially by UKIP, increased the prejudice, deliberately inciting hostility to all foreigners. The referendum on Europe and the processes in Brexit have demonstrated that feelings of superiority and hostility extend to our European neighbours.

The Home Office's illegal 'hostile environment' over the decades has ruined lives, and continues to do so. Theresa May is largely identified as the cause of the Windrush Scandal with her 'hostile environment'. But Professor David Olusoga researched government records to show that successive governments, Labour and Tory, had been equally racist. Even after asking for help from the colonies, governments never intended or expected the colonists to settle here. After the Second World War, while immigrants from the Caribbean were being refused, ex-Nazis from

Europe were being encouraged to settle here.

The government's treatment of British commonwealth citizens and refugees of all sorts has been shameful. The cruelty and incompetence shown by the Windrush scandal and the way colonial troops have been treated, continues to persecute the vulnerable. Priti Patel fits the same abusive pattern. Typically, she makes a distinction between those who can afford to come legally (the very wealthy) who are acceptable, and those coming without the right 'papers' which inevitably includes anyone fleeing war, persecution or starvation, who are deemed illegal. Does she really think people in those situations have any chance of getting the right papers?

At the same time, because refugees are not allowed to contribute while their cases are being heard, and this often takes a very long time, the policy has been and remains very expensive as well as being bad for the refugees' health and mental state.

Very recently Boris Johnson made his contempt for international law crystal clear with his proposal to override the withdrawal agreement with the EU, as well as proposals to exempt British soldiers from being charged with war crimes.

Regarding international law, the UK can best be described as a rogue state.

Chapter 5   The Importance of Status, Trident

As our real power faded after the 2nd World War, the importance of hanging on to our earlier perceived status in the world, built on colonialism, military might and commercial success, became a major feature of policy. Among many other things it dominated our 'defence' policy, including our determination to remain a nuclear power.

Support for Trident is a perfect example of the obsession with global status by successive governments which has poisoned political life and society in general. Bruce Kent pointed out at a meeting several years ago in Norwich that Atlee's government insisted on our own bomb not for defence as is claimed now, but out of pique that America would not share its secrets with us, deeming us unsafe. Similarly, Polaris was adopted to keep up with the French nuclear programme. In both cases it was clearly about status.

Retaining Trident follows the same pattern. There can be no logical reason for keeping a weapon which is a major threat to our survival. Status, the wish to be aligned with America and investments for some, must underlie support for Trident. The arguments made and the lack of information shared show a gross failure of our democracy.

'World in Chains', based on recent research, describes the system and its dangers. Trident consists of 4 submarines, with up to 8 missiles and no more than 40 warheads per submarine. Each warhead can be specifically targeted and each delivers 100Kt destructive power. In comparison, the atomic bomb over Hiroshima delivered 18kt. The missiles from one submarine contain more destructive power than all the bombs of the 2nd World War, including the atom bombs dropped on Hiroshima and Nagasaki.

As a weapon of mass destruction, it is designed to create maximum amounts of damage, death and injury and designed to be targeted at large cities. If ever used, millions of people would be maimed, burned, blinded or poisoned. Large areas would remain dangerously radioactive for several years. Communications and electronic systems that control the electric grid, water supplies and traffic control, would be inoperative.

Wherever it is targeted, swift climatic cooling would lead to a nuclear winter over the entire northern hemisphere which could lead to about 2 billion deaths from famine. The use of just one missile would overwhelm the medical resources of a country. The combined firepower of the 40 missiles on one Trident submarine has the power to unleash a global apocalypse.

Trident is a genocidal and suicidal weapon of mass destruction which affects enemies and allies alike. No rational person could use it in any circumstances.   His Excellency Judge Mohammed Bedjaoui, former President of the International Court of Justice at The Hague, wrote in 2011 that the overwhelming and indiscriminate destructive power of Trident made any use in any circumstance illegal and that having the system was illegal.

Yet in the face of this evidence, and the protests of thousands of people over decades, successive governments and the media continue to describe Trident as our 'independent nuclear deterrent', even sometimes our 'minimum' deterrent. To their shame the church supported the myth last year, holding a thanksgiving ceremony for 50 years of Peace.

We should think about the word 'deterrent'. It sounds safe and sensible. The way to avoid trouble. A lot of solicitors' work aims to deter potential trouble by foreseeing complications.   In personal life we admire someone who can stand up for themselves. Someone one would not 'mess' with. But this is within reason. It has to be proportionate. This is true in law as well where self defence is allowed, and criminal damage is allowed if it is to stop greater harm. But it has to be proportionate.

This is true for war and we understand this principle in our personal lives. A strong person is valued. But a bully is avoided. You would not choose to try to co-operate or deal with a bully. And, critically, anyone threatening to kill or maim to protect themselves from potential threats and developing the means to do so, would be arrested or committed to an asylum. Yet this is precisely what our independent nuclear weapons does. It threatens catastrophe for completely unidentified and unspecified potential threats.

Governments' claims have been lies and unsubstantiated assumptions. Trident is not 'independent'. The missiles are American. Their use depends on American agreement. There is no evidence that Trident has 'deterred' anything. There is no evidence that anyone has wanted to attack us. Indeed why would they want to when they can take us over so easily by 'investing' in businesses here or buying large amounts of property here? They will almost certainly be given grants or tax inducements to do so. Countries without nuclear weapons have not suffered invasions. At the same time there has been no peace. Wars have continued in which our soldiers are dying, while terrorists kill civilians here.

The Non-Proliferation Treaty signed in 1968 recognised the essential danger of nuclear weapons. It asked countries not to adopt them on the condition that the nuclear powers get rid of theirs. Since then successive government in nuclear countries have failed to honour this agreement. While claiming to be in favour of multi-lateral disarmament they have failed to act. Instead they have made the contradictory and incoherent claim that our nuclear weapons keep us safe but it would be dangerous for other countries to have it. We must keep ours but they mustn't get any. This could only be true if we, the nuclear nations, were completely competent and completely wise, in contrast to non-nuclear states. But there is no evidence to support this view.

Over the decades, both governments and the media have also confused the situation by contrasting multi- and uni-lateral disarmament. Multi - good, uni -bad. The claim that we need to keep Trident as a bargaining chip in multi-lateral negotiations is nonsense. Trident, terrible though it is, is nothing compared to the arsenals of the US and Russia. It will be quite irrelevant in those negotiation. Bi-lateral agreements will be needed there and we have no power to influence them.

However, on the global scale, we have a chance to influence other countries positively. Having Trident encourages proliferation. As long as we continue to claim it protects us we cannot expect others not to think the same. Indeed, countries such as North Korea and Israel may well reasonably feel their nuclear weapons save them from attack. That for them they are a 'deterrent'.

If we 'unilaterally' gave up Trident this would at least reduce the danger to everyone from our own weapons, and so help to reduce some global tension. It would also help multi-lateral nuclear disarmament by dissuading other potential nuclear states and reminding nuclear powers of the dangers and the costs. We could make honest arguments about the dangers.

There was a chance to put Trident on the table in multi-lateral talks at the UN Conference on Prohibiting Nuclear Weapons in 2017, but Mrs May's government demonstrated its unwillingness to consider disarmament of any sort by not even attending. Mrs May, the first prime minister to boast that she would press the red button, seemed more determined than ever to keep our missiles. She endorsed Trident very early in her term. She had a statement read out in Parliament which reneged on our previous commitment to international law with regards to our nuclear weapons which made nuclear attack more likely and hampered nuclear disarmament. And she supported the expansion of nuclear power when there is no justification for it as an energy source.

Boris Johnson has gone even further by proposing an increase in nuclear missiles. It just gets worse.

The present situation breaks our own military rules. No commander is meant to fire without knowing the consequences and considering civilian losses. But the missiles are targeted by computer, so the men on the submarine have no idea where they will go or what damage they will cause.

Perhaps most worrying, all governments have ignored the very high risk of accidental use. Trident is the least democratic of weapons. Firing it relies on perfectly functioning computer systems and very few people. Those involved have to remain rational while making split second decisions at a time of tension. We know computers go wrong all too often. We know people go mad, particularly at times of tension. Accidents, horrific accidents, are a common feature of life. Several near accidents have already occurred with nuclear weapons.

Over recent years, the existence of suicidal terrorists means the logic of Mutually Assured Destruction, MAD, which was assumed to deter any use, no longer applies. In the face of suicide bombings, we can no longer assume that people always want to survive and so will be 'sensible'.

The increase in sophisticated cybercrime also increases the danger. We know the security services have not always managed to identify potential attackers. In addition, previous hot lines between opposing countries to allow essential contact at times of tension no longer exist.

Several voices, including the analysts of the Doomsday Clock, have been warning us for years of the increased danger in having these weapons. Some say it is not a matter of 'if' there will be an accident, but 'when'. Our governments have been criminally negligent to ignore them.

It is important to realise that the media, including the BBC, have colluded with the government to support Trident. Earlier debates when the Labour Party was considering rejecting nuclear weapons have been long forgotten. None of Mrs May's actions were questioned, while Jeremy Corbyn was ridiculed for opposing nuclear weapons. Over the decades thousands of protesters have continued to demonstrate regularly in a variety of ways, many willing to go to jail, but very little of this has been shared with the public, and certainly not their arguments.

In my own recent experience, in 2015 a legal attempt launched by hundreds of people to get the dangers of Trident debated in court in a Public Interest Action Against Trident (PICAT) was ignored by local and national media. Over 250 people in the Norwich area signed the court papers, but the local paper did not deign to report its presentation at the Magistrates Court in Norwich. And this was not on a big news day. As far as I know only Scottish papers covered the issue. The Attorney General refused to allow the case to be heard. Who knows whether that would have happened had the press given it full coverage?

It is no exaggeration to state that those thousands of whistle blowers trying to alert the general public and MPs to the dangers and costs of Trident have been gagged, while the official 'debate' for several decades now has depended on lies, incoherent arguments, false assumptions and a disregard for international and domestic law. It is truly shocking that so many MPs have been content to mouth platitudes and not investigate the real facts. In my experience, even seemingly caring MPs when given the evidence, have chosen to leave the issue to defence spokesperson.

If they are so complacent or misinformed about such a vital policy, we must wonder if they are any better informed about other matters. And, what chance is there for the general public to be well informed, while the thousands of whistle blowers are frustrated and demoralised? This long term cancer at the heart of policy making has inevitably degraded political life, not to mention the huge waste of money and lost opportunities. Our nuclear 'defence' policy is a continuing democratic disaster as well as a hazard to world peace.

Chapter 6   Capitalism

Capitalism is usually claimed by Western countries to go hand in hand with democracy.   Both together lauded as the 'free' world, giving opportunity, choice, prosperity and individual freedom in contrast to the dead hand and central control of communism.

Perhaps, given the characteristics of advertising and spin, we should not be surprised that the opposite is true. Capitalism is directly opposed to, and incompatible with, democratic values and aims. It is driven by debt and consumerism. It exists in a parallel world of accountants, banks and businesses where money and profits are all that matters. And where the rules are made to suit themselves but are treated as if laws of nature.

Capitalism interlinked with business practices directly undermines democracy. The commercial confidentiality, contracts, cover ups and gagging orders, all of which are a necessary part of competition between businesses, stop the transparency and accountability essential for democratic control and co-operation.

Capitalism undermines governments through unelected credit rating agencies and the unaccountable banking system, which control a country's ability to borrow and the terms of the payback. This has been particularly disastrous for developing countries in the South. The rules set by undemocratic, capitalist global institutions including Wall Street, the World Bank(WB), the International Monetary Fund (IMF) and the World Trade Organisation (WTO) have been rigged to favour rich Western countries.

Decades ago, many poor countries which had started to recover from the ravages of colonialism, needed loans because oil prices and interest rates had rocketed. To access these loans they were forced by the World Bank to spend on privatisation and industrial projects which suited the donors, instead of the social services they needed. The 'austerity' imposed in this way became the major cause of poverty in the South since colonialism. It made it impossible for national governments to follow policies they and their populations wanted. Capitalism effectively destroyed democracy.

Capitalism has always been blatantly unfair. The basic system by which the poorer you are the higher interest you pay, while the seriously rich can live on the earnings of their money without doing a stroke of work, is designed to make the rich richer and keep the poor poorer. This applies to both individuals and countries. The 'trickle down' theory long used as a justification has been proved wrong. The opposite has happened; a trickle up leading to greater and greater inequality.

In this country the punitive ratcheting up debts if they are not paid quickly and the extra costs of court hearings and bailiffs all work to maintain poverty. Globally, inequality between the South and north has tripled since the 1960s.

Globally, the poor countries, receive a huge amount in aid, $130 billion annually, from rich countries, but this is dwarfed by far greater sums of money and resources flowing north. It has been calculated that for every $1 the South receives in aid, $24 dollars flow the other way. Jason Hickel also describes how the system of compound interest means countries have repaid the debt many times, but still owe money. There is even a method of stealing money through falsifying trade invoices, legalised by WTO in 1994. Money which can then be hidden in tax havens.

Within countries and between countries the inequality and poverty it causes has led to countless refugees as well as increased division and hatred in the world. Capitalism must be a significant cause of today's crime, war, migration and extremism. The hopes and aspirations of millions of people, quite apart from their basic need to survive, cannot be denied for decades without some reaction - either violence and guerrilla warfare for revenge, or migration to escape hunger, poverty or unemployment.

A new under class 'the precariat' has been identified. People failed by governments, pushed into long term insecurity by punitive social conditions such as unemployment, insecure jobs, housing crises, war, starvation, etc. The precariat have no stake in society because it offers them nothing. They are a destabilising force. Some may be tempted by the far right and criminal gangs into destructive actions, both in the UK and abroad.

A fatal flaw in capitalism is its need for continuous growth. Simply impossible in a finite world. Over the decades nations and businesses have exploited natural resources causing massive pollution and degradation of the environment. It has now reached the stage when the natural life of the world on which we all depend is threatened by mass extinction and a broken climate.

Another aspect of capitalism, and one almost always ignored, is the fact that it undermines the family. The family for all its faults, has for centuries been a basic unit of social organisation and cohesion. Capitalism directly threatens the family and all types of voluntary work, by only recognising paid work as having any value.

As a direct result, the care of children has suffered. In the UK through the policies of successive monetarist governments with the help of the media and even feminism, the idea of caring for children, relatives and friends has been downgraded. As far back as the 1970s, when I was looking after my four children on my own – a very big job - I remember the constant refrain 'only a housewife'.

Since then, with rising house prices and lower wages, both parents have often been forced into paid work. Even frivolous, damaging or polluting paid work is valued above caring for their own. Many families have been forced to neglect their children against their will. It has led among many other examples, to the cruel position where a family can get no help to look after a disabled child at home, but if the child is looked after by others, as a job, they will be well paid.

Today, the importance of money rather than the welfare of family, particularly children, is illustrated in many polices. By the way immigrants are not allowed to have their family members join them unless they are very wealthy. By punishing poorer families by restricting child allowance to just two children and the bedroom tax. By making young people pay for further education.

The triumph of heartless capitalism over common humanity and loving relationships is demonstrated today by all those leaders and wealthy people who still pursue damaging 'business as usual' and those who support therm. They are all deliberately choosing to steal their own children's futures.

We should not be surprised that capitalism produces a harsh and punitive society. In biblical terms, it is the embodiment of several vices, greed, laziness, envy, selfishness, lack of compassion. Such harshness is not unusual or exclusive to capitalism. Throughout history many systems of organisation from monarchy to colonialism, have allowed the privileged to exploit others. Cruelty and inhumanity are common. Capitalism is the modern way to exploit. Unfortunately, it has been so successful that it has cut the ground from under its own feet, putting all life in danger. The ideals of democracy stand in contrast. It aims to be fair to all, ruled by good laws chosen by all, on behalf of all.

When looking to the future we must challenge the myth that capitalism is the only way to organise society, communism having failed. We must recognise that both capitalism and communism are flawed. They were both systems devised by people, not laws of the universe. At this critical time, when the systems we have used are clearly failing, we have to create a system suited to the circumstances. It is clear that to survive together we urgently need a system that enables and encourages co-operation between very different cultures to solve common global problems.

Chapter 7   The Influence of Capitalism on UK Policies.

How has our 'democratic' political system dealt with capitalism? A few decades ago, the norm for many households was to have one earner, probably in the capitalist world or in the service sector, with a wife at home to care for the family. The two systems co-existed. The ills of capitalism, within the country, were counteracted by socialist welfare. A safety net. Since then capitalism has increased its dominance with support from the major political parties.

The present dire state of affairs had its origins decades ago in the government of Margaret Thatcher. Critically, she introduced neoliberal free market economic policies in contrast to the earlier Keynesian view. Neoliberals claim that market forces alone produce the best conditions for living. Their policies are largely carried out through the privatisation of services. They favour low taxes, low wages for the majority but certainly not for all, and deregulation, including deregulation of the financial sector. The Big Bang, made banking a global activity and changed its nature. This almost certainly caused the banking crash of 2008.

This economic policy coincided with, and was linked to, a hatred of local government, trades unions, professionals and 'community'. Magaret Thatcher was famous for saying there was no such thing as 'society'. Over time the central control over policies has drastically reduced participation at local levels of government, and as a consequence, the information available to central government. Tiers of local government were, and are still, faced with impossible situations with less power and money but often more demanding tasks.

Today much of local government is 'democratic' in name only. The situation depends on the individuals involved. Proactive councillors can make a real difference, but in my experience, in many cases information and debate are lacking and communication between layers of government non-existent. Party politics controls decisions, which are taken at prior meetings behind closed doors.

Representation has been further eroded as more decisions are made by 'cabinets' or delegated to officers, quite apart from the number made by unelected quangos. At the same time the number of MPs and Councillors has been reduced.

Thatcher attacked three basic policies central to decent standards of social life; housing, education and health.

As far back as the 1950s the importance of decent housing, with enough space and facilities was recognised as vital for the wellbeing of tenants. Improved standards were adopted by the Ministry of Housing for all council houses. But with neoliberal ideas, housing became an investment rather than a home. Allowing council tenants to buy their properties was a tempting bribe to individual families, an appeal to their aspirations and for their votes, but It began the destruction of social housing.

The introduction of private landlords led fairly directly over time to the disastrous conditions of today: high rents, lack of security for tenants, a severe housing shortage, overcrowded poor quality houses, homelessness and the continuing tragedies of Grenfell and many similar housing projects.

When councils were no longer responsible for building houses for rent, these also were built for profit not providing homes, which contributed significantly to the lack of suitable housing today.

Education similarly became a business rather than a service, with far greater central control. It was taken away from the control of local councils with grant maintained schools and tech colleges funded from central government. Schools were made to compete in a market, and a national curriculum imposed. Teachers were no longer trusted.

I started teaching then and could not help but notice the rage of older teachers, who, feeling utterly despised, were no longer willing to carry out the many out of hours voluntary clubs they had supported so willingly before – chess clubs, sports events. At the time I thought the attack on education was deliberate and typical of an advertising agency – Saatchi & Saatchi. Thatcher didn't want people, particularly from state schools, to be able to think and criticise her policies.

Her lack of care for children's wellbeing was shown by cutting free school milk and selling off sports fields, in the name of efficiency. This was in tune with her declaration that community did not exist. Individual ambition was all. Social action, friendliness and altruism, the glue of social cohesion, were no longer valued.

Her legacy can be seen in today's education market - privatised school trusts and free schools, with large class sizes, and overburdened teachers having to follow an exacting curriculum poor in the arts. While at the same time having to prove their worth through endless assessments and box ticking. This in contrast to the so called public schools for those who can afford them, with much smaller classes and better facilities, which are treated as charities.

Her treatment of universities was compared at the time to Henry VIII's dissolution of the monasteries with deeper cuts than any other public service, while academics lost their secure jobs. A couple of years ago I heard some lecturers were on zero hour controls. The market has become so central to the survival of universities that news of commercial links dominates graduation days and presumably control their policies. Also cuts in direct government funding mean that universities have to rely on student numbers which almost certainly skews admission policy in general.

In the NHS Margaret Thatcher started the changes that have been carried on by successive governments. She forced it to use an 'internal market'. Health authorities no longer ran hospitals but instead had to 'purchase' care from hospitals competing with others to provide it. They became independent, self-governing trusts. All this in the name of efficiency and to eliminate waste through competition.

Privatisation became the goals both in drug development and services. It transformed the NHS into a 'business', with profits for providers its main aim; and with the added commercial problems of secrecy, covering up mistakes, legal costs and patents. Private companies could 'cherry pick' the more profitable treatments. The result - a huge increase in costs with much of the money going to private providers and layers of management.

Critically, the demand for quick profits by businesses has led to a lack of research into long term projects, such as the need for new anti-biotics. Warnings have continued for years that these are needed as resistance develops to existing treatments, but the drug companies are not interested. This sort of research cannot be left to market forces.

In the development of drugs, medicines largely discovered and developed with taxpayer-funded research, were patented at a late stage by major pharmaceutical companies, who then charged the NHS high fees. An example of stripping state assets in favour of private businesses.

The huge financial power of pharmaceutical companies has enabled them to invest millions in advertising and political lobbying, shaping policy to increase their profits, funding candidates that support their position, funding biased trials, even falsely attributing comments to eminent researchers and influencing doctors to prescribe specific drugs. Corruption has been endemic.

The close alliance between drug companies and MPs ideologically in favour of market forces adds to the problem. In February 2017 a list of 62 MPs was published with links to private healthcare medical firms.

Three other factors; centrally imposed levels of management and targets for treatment and screening; PFI projects (Private Financed Initiatives) to set up PPPs (Public-Private Partnerships) favoured investors and imposed high long term costs on the taxpayer; austerity cuts in funding for pay and facilities and the lack of training grants, have all added to the costs and woes of the NHS.

The changes promoted as 'efficiency savings' have proved to be the opposite, with high costs, long waiting times, unnecessary deaths, poor recovery rates, broken targets, understaffing, stress among health professionals and expensive agency staff, all plaguing the service – and that was before the horror of Covid19!

Today, the NHS can no longer boast of being one of the most successful health services. Its performance lags behind those of other developed countries. Doctors and nurses are unable to deliver the service they would want to, having also largely lost their right to decide on the best treatment. In too many cases, in this stressed situation, patients are processed by 'pathways' like inanimate objects, rather than respected as people.

The changes Thatcher started were accompanied by attacks on the Trades Unions, described as 'the enemy within'. Trades Unions were stripped of their legal protection. Striking, the most effective way by which most working people can protect themselves, was made harder. Heavy industry, the mines, steel works, shipbuilding, the car industry were all allowed to fail. Thatcher removed the regional financial support which might have saved them.

Her aim was to rely on service industries in the UK, and get goods manufactured abroad where labour costs were much lower. "It was a conscious policy," said Graham Stringer, a Labour MP at the time. An attack on manufacturing as the basis for the Labour party and labour movement. Competition from outsourcing work abroad where labour laws were weaker and labour much cheaper, was a threat to working people's incomes here.

The result was the worst recession since the 1930s between 1981 and 1983, destroying one fifth of our industrial base and doubling unemployment, even before war was declared on the miners. In 1983, one in six of Scotland's workers was on the dole and the number of unemployed under-25s had doubled to 1.5million. With a similar story in England and Wales whole communities were destroyed.

Thatcher's policies can be seen as class warfare. Her 'reforms' did not impinge on the wealthy who owned their own houses, could afford private schools and health care and for the most part did not work in heavy industry. Her government began the wholesale overthrow of democracy in favour of capitalist institutions through privatisation. Other parties have largely carried on her work, with Tony Blair's 'the third way', and the Lib Dems in coalition with the Tories.

Overall her policies have moved British politics, among many others, far to the right. It was a probably no coincidence that neoliberalism gained influence just as communism was seen to fail. At the time, I admired Gorbachev's attempt to reform the Soviet Union. I still have a copy of his speech to the UN, as he alone seemed to behave as a global statesman. I regret that the West chose not to make use of a potential peace dividend, but instead chose triumphalism.

Capitalism is the common choice of the democratic western world, but I suggest that in the UK (and the US) the more extreme neoliberal ideas - Selfish Capitalism - developed more easily because of historic class distinctions – including slavery. Capitalism with its winners and losers fits in the UK with the exploitation accepted by our class ideology and our history of colonisation.

Over the last decade, the close relationship between the Conservatives and big business, on which the Tory party depends for its finance, has been increased by a revolving door between industrial jobs and MPs, countless corporate 'advisers' in Parliament and MPs investments in corporations. Business and government speak with one voice and share the declared aim to 'shrink government', a euphemism for 'shrink democracy'. They are supported in this aim by the other large businesses involved in the media. Our so-called democracy has effectively become a Plutocracy - rule by the elite for the elite, with no heed for the majority.

Chapter 8 – Transport, a major policy influenced by privatisation, distrust of unions and support for fossil fuels

Ever since the second world war, road, the most polluting form, has been favoured over rail. This was driven by hostility to, and fear of, the railway trades unions since the general strike in 1926. And by the large number of unemployed service men who had learnt to drive, along with countless army HGVs available at the end of the war. It was convenient to use road freight to solve both these problems, especially as the railways were expensive to maintain and had fallen into disrepair during the war.

The Beeching cuts compounded the damage. The cuts were all about saving money in the short term. Buses were supposed to be an adequate substitute for unprofitable lines. No thought of was given to possible changes in the future which rail could serve, nor to the huge waste of capital investment in the lines. The aim was to make the railways profitable. This soon failed and subsidies were needed.

The result was catastrophic for many rural areas, where bus services were poor. In my North Norfolk village in the late 60s and 70s people reminisced sadly on the loss of their local line. You used to be able to flag the train down at the level crossing across the field. On Saturdays the women went to Norwich to shop, the men to football and a late train brought them back after the pubs closed. It sounded civilised.

Today, when many more people want to use rail, a complicated privatisation has proved a disaster, leading to one of the most expensive services in Europe, with overcrowded, unreliable trains, plagued by strikes and unhelpful complicated ticketing and two major accidents. Commuters lives have been made a misery, while many people are priced out of using rail.

Electrification has reduced the use of diesel but has sometimes been halted after much expense for lack of funds, for example at Bristol.

The controversial HS2 line which is destroying precious woodlands and countryside at a time when nobody knows what future transport needs will be, shows the government's priority for speed and large status projects rather than concern for the climate, the environment and local connections.

Road policy has proved no better. Expensive road building programmes and faster roads, particularly in the absence of adequate rail and bus services, led to a huge increase in private cars, with its associated pollution, congestion, parking problems and alarming numbers of deadly accidents. Bypasses, usually advocated to cure pollution and congestion, have more often led to more car dependent housing on the outskirts of towns, leading to even further pollution and congestion. By late 2017 85% of UK "air quality zones" still exceeded legal pollution limits eight years after they were supposed to meet them, (National Audit Office).

Since then the government has continued to poison the air. In contradiction to the claimed policies of the 'polluter pays' and 'combating climate change'; the documented effects of air pollution on health; and the threat of EU fines and court cases, air pollution seems of no concern to the present government. They are still planning more roads, and have for several years frozen the duty on petrol which aimed to discourage car use and encourage cycling and walking.

The car industry has always been seen as a major asset. It is now one of the few manufacturing sectors left. However, the cars made here are now largely for foreign owners. The profits go abroad while tax breaks and development grants are funded by the tax payer to tempt foreign companies to come here and give British workers jobs. In 2019 ut was revealed that Theresa May had offered Nissan a £61 million aid package to stay here after Brexit. This was kept secret at the time.

In addition, air traffic, the most polluting form of transport, is exempt from VAT and fuel duty. Flights, much cheaper than expensive rail, are driving higher carbon emissions. Tax exemption was agreed internationally in 1944 to encourage the early development of air traffic. Since then the number of flights has increased dramatically. International air traffic is the fastest growing sector of pollution. The need for adequate taxation now is obvious. The EU is committed to work for a new international agreement and has allowed domestic flights to be taxed since 1996, but governments in the UK have failed to take advantage of this.

International tourism is a major factor in increasing air traffic. Mass tourism is unsustainable in many other ways. A major factor in producing quite unnecessary amounts of cheap 'stuff', often plastic, destroying many natural habitats, and producing mountains of waste. The needs of local populations are ignored in the rush to lure tourists. One small example, in Majorca, as far back as the 70s, water ran short for local people, who had to buy it shipped in, while hoses ran freely to grow luscious plants in town centres and round hotels. And the island was overcome with waste.

(However, I take the point Simon Reeves makes that controlled eco-tourism to support environmental projects can be helpful both to maintain them and to educate the rest of us.)

In addition, many of our other domestic policies and planning decisions have increased traffic. Local schools and hospitals have been closed in favour of fewer larger ones. Supermarkets, out of town shopping centres, and car dependent edge of town housing developments have all led to more traffic.

Finally, the destruction of our manufacturing sector has led to a huge increase in shipping as the products we need are made overseas, and our waste, too, is shipped abroad. Yet neither shipping nor air traffic emissions are included in UK official carbon figures, a case of creative accounting noted by Greta Thunberg.

Chapter 9 – Energy, another major policy affected by privatisation and support for fossil fuels

Privatisation and the market philosophy are not the only problems in the energy sector. The government's energy policy has defied all logic. Instead of making use of our own natural resources to produce cheap reliable, renewable and safe energy it has supported expensive, polluting and dangerous alternatives, with profits often going abroad.

With the best wind resource in Europe, and turbines already highly developed by the aircraft industry, wind power has been available for decades and would be the quickest way to cut carbon. As long ago as the 70s the Lucas Plan devised by shop stewards suggested producing turbines as a socially useful product to save their jobs as arms production declined.

Onshore wind power is the cheapest and easiest to produce. A worldwide survey suggests that with the latest improvements onshore wind is now cheaper by over £20.00 per megawatt hour than gas or coal fired stations, and considerably cheaper than nuclear production. The price can only get cheaper with further development.

It is also the form of electricity that best suits the grid. To ensure supply at peak times, there has to be excess available to be switched on and off as required. Wind turbines are the best system for fluctuating demand. When nuclear power stations go down, as happens quite regularly, this is a nightmare for the grid operatives.

Wind power, as with any source, is most efficient when produced nearest to where it is being used. As single turbines are relatively cheap, it is very suitable for small community projects. More reasons why on-shore wind is best, producing the cheapest energy and supporting the local economy.

Despite this evidence, or more likely because of it, the government has worked to make onshore wind power extremely difficult to install, if not impossible. Investors are deterred by expensive pre-planning surveys - apparently more than those needed for nuclear plants. The situation is made worse because the MOD can veto a project at the last minute, and usually gives no definite answer during the pre-planning stage.

In the case of a community wind project I was involved in, the MOD did worse. It broke a firm commitment to allow a turbine, given several years previously with no caveats, by vetoing it at the moment of applying for planning permission, wasting years of work by volunteers and £1000s from local investors and the organisations that gave us grants. (When I rang the person who had been dealing with us all along and had given the written assurances, she promised to sort it out. But the next time I rang she had been moved.)

In addition, subsidies to wind have been slashed, while those to fossil fuels remained. David Cameron claimed the UK needed no more onshore wind, and the government aimed to ban it. Despite majority public support for onshore wind shown by many surveys, the government has effectively destroyed the UK onshore wind industry. They have been aided by aggressive local campaigns by climate change deniers, spreading scaremongering misinformation. In the case of our community wind project it did not stop at lies. The farmer and his family were threatened and the met mast to record speeds was vandalised.

The government's hostility to on-shore wind does nothing for the good of the public or the planet. By failing to use our best natural resource, the only winners have been the fossil fuel companies, nuclear energy and their investors.

The government supports off-shore wind. This is both more expensive and less efficient than on-shore production because of the electricity lost in transmission and the costly work required for installation and maintenance. Critically, off shore wind can only be undertaken by large corporations or governments. These are mostly foreign owned so the profits go abroad.

The government appeared to support solar energy for a short while. This is far less efficient than wind in our climate, guaranteed not to work when we need lights and to be extremely inefficient in winter. Early subsidies, which jump-started a surge in local businesses installing panels, were soon slashed, and the future plan seems to be to pay nothing for the electricity exported to the grid – effectively robbing those with panels and undermining the industry.

In accordance with its stated policy to cut carbon emissions in accordance with the Paris agreement, the government promised to get rid of the remaining eight coal fired power plants by 2025. However continuing subsidies for coal will go on customers' bills, and Ministers can restore coal if they feel it is necessary. Contradicting this policy, it has recently re-opened an old coal mining site and is considering a second one.

Furthermore, the government's support for fracking completely undermines the cuts in coal, while showing contempt for the public's views. Oil and gas for heating and transport also continue to be subsidised and very recently new licenses have been granted in the North Sea.

The worst aspect of government energy policy is its support for nuclear power, the most expensive and the most dangerous means of production, with the additional problem of a bad track record of delays. The unsolved problem of how to store the waste safely for generations to come should be enough to ban nuclear power. It is completely immoral to impose the unknown dangers and unknown costs of our electricity on our children, grandchildren, great grandchildren and further generations. On 17 November 2020 the Guardian reported that that the Nuclear Decommissioning Authority (NDA) admitted to MPs that it still does not fully know the condition of its sites, including 10 closed Magnox stations from Dungeness in Kent to Hunterston in Ayrshire. A recent estimate is that decommissioning will cost £132billion over the next 120 years.

Using new models of reactors adds to the uncertainty. We are effectively guinea pigs taking all the risks, with EDF and the Chinese taking the profits.

The claim that nuclear power is renewable and will not cause carbon emissions is extremely dubious. Long term storage has not been part of the equation. And building the sites needs enormous amounts of concrete and other materials which entail significant carbon emissions up front now, exactly when we need to cut back drastically.

The real reason for supporting nuclear energy is most likely to be its link to nuclear weapons, but the excuse is that it provides a constant baseline of electricity, as opposed to fluctuating wind. However, the UK is well endowed with renewables to provide this. Tidal and wave power would together produce a benign renewable baseline source. Cancelling the Swansea barrage, while supporting nuclear power and fracking demonstrates the government's dangerous ideological priorities.

The government claims to be in favour of cheap electricity. People are continuously encouraged to use market forces and switch suppliers to get the best de. But this is a smoke screen when the government has guaranteed a very high price for nuclear power, to be paid by customers. Also a significant part of the price is the cost of carrying the electricity by UK Power Networks, a monopoly. While, changing policy on wood burners and aerobic digesters is incoherent.

Chapter 10   Fossil fuels and synthetic pesticides in Intensive Farming and Food Production

The falsely named 'green' revolution which promised cheap food and larger crops was a deadly illusion. In just over 70 years it has destroyed the healthy soils produced by hundreds of years of traditional farming using crop rotation and natural manure.   Intensive agriculture has hastened global warming by the use of oil based fertilisers, by increasing food miles, by deforestation and by eliminating hedge rows to accommodate huge machinery which also compact the soil.

The synthetic pesticides used are a danger to the ecosystems on which we rely for survival. They have polluted our environment, destroyed our soils, and killed insects and other organisms to such an extent that we now have a worldwide extinction of species.   Monocultures have reduced diversity on the land and increased the risk of disease in the crop.

Globally, Genetically Modified crops are the worst aspect of modern farming techniques. A frightening example of man's arrogance. His belief he can control nature. Lauded as the 'answer' to food supplies for a growing world population, it is in fact a huge danger to natural life but the perfect prize for any business. What could be better for continuing profits than controlling a staple food – something we all need every day?

Most of my early information comes from talks given in 2004 during a local public consultation on GM crops by John Latham, Helena Paul and Peter Melchett. Their comments are still relevant today.   My later information comes from the amazing work of Vandana Shiva in India.

John Latham, a plant geneticist, disproved the claim that GM technology is a highly accurate way of speeding up the natural breeding programme. Genetic analysis of GM plants showed that the physical damage caused by shooting DNA, often contaminated DNA, into cells, with the tissue cultures used and other processes, introduces hundreds or even thousands of changes, such that the GM plant is halfway to being another species – often with surprising characteristics and ones that are not understood.

John also described very lax regulation, quoting a letter from the American Food and Drug administration (FDA) to Monsanto about a new corn variety. The letter had 'no further questions' about a GM variety which had 60 times less Beta Carotene, twice as much Vitamin A, 10% less iron and $4^{1/}_2$ times as much Sodium. John commented that Monsanto must have known something about the FDA to have risked presenting this extraordinary material. An example of lax regulation in the UK, was a test for the safety of Charden LL maize, which showed statistically, by 80%, the product was dangerous. The chickens died. Yet it was passed.

Contamination of other crops by neighbouring GM crops is a huge problem. Farmers reported that by 2003 it was impossible to grow organic oil seed rape in Saskatchewan. And in North Dakota an organic farmer lost a large contract for organic soya because it was contaminated.

GM crops, it was claimed, would solve the problems of the third world, increasing yields and making the lives of farmers easier, by avoiding weeding. The opposite has proved true. Yields have been lower and local farmers after a few years have experienced herbicide resistance. In Argentina spraying from aeroplanes was reported to cause sickness in children and the death of small animals.

Vandana Shiva describes the situation in India where thousands of diverse communities have traditionally made their living from the natural world around them. In return they have sustained the natural environment. This symbiotic relationship comes from a deep knowledge of nature that has evolved over centuries to produce all the requirements for life, including medicines and food in many different climate conditions.

All this is threatened by what she calls 'Biopiracy', the Western imposition of IPRs (Intellectual Property Rights) allowing patenting for the benefit of Transnational Corporations (TNCs). GM companies have in effect stolen the rich peasant knowledge of foods, medicinal herbs, natural pesticides and preservatives and different animal breeds by using it as their own private property, often after very small changes. They make big profits from their patents, while the overwhelming contributions of the original farmers are ignored. Also, critically, the traditional free flow of seeds and knowledge essential for traditional systems of farming and medicine are blocked.

'Terminator seeds' make farmers totally dependent on GM companies, obeying their complicated planting and growing regimes and suffering their price rises. In 2019 Vandana Shiva described the tragedy of 310,000 suicides in India caused by poverty among farmers, mostly those sowing Monsanto's BT Cotton. This cotton was meant to provide protection from a common pest, but over the years the pest became immune. Monsanto increased the price of their seed by 80,000%. When the seed companies refused to collect royalties, Monsanto sued falsely claiming that they had a patent. Vandana Shiva was involved in the court case where Monsanto tried, but failed in that case to overturn India's law.

GM has had a tragic effect on the third world because it has more biodiversity and more farmers. In their pursuit of ownership, corporations have patented countless plant varieties. As Helena Paul insists, GM is all about the control of food supplies and seed, for profit. She described solutions to counter pests and diseases and increase yields that work with nature. But, because these benign solutions cannot be patented, businesses will not invest in them, nor will governments who believe in the market support them.

American law has tightened the hold of their corporations. The American 1996 Economic Espionage Act, criminalised the natural development and exchange of knowledge. It allowed intelligence agencies to investigate farmers and growers to protect the rights of GM companies. Early examples come from America and Canada. In 2003, the late Peter Melchett, then head of the Soil Association, reported that hundreds of American farmers found Pinkerton's agents, paid by Monsanto, inspecting their farms for potential GM crops.

In one case they claimed to have found GM Soya when the crop was sugar beet. Any settlements agreed had to be kept secret. As already mentioned, the problem was in fact the other way round. Contamination by GM crops was costing organic farmers lost contracts.

The Special 301 clause of the US Trade Regulations, puts the interests of the GM corporations above all else. A country unwilling to accept GM crops can be forced by the power of the IMF and the World Bank to change national laws to protect the profits of GM companies.

The corporations pursuing GM, supported by the UK and US governments, continue to make exaggerated claims for them, and try to evade restrictions by slightly altering the process. The newest gene drive technology presents an even greater threat.

Intensive animal farming of all sorts – whether pork, beef, chicken or salmon, with the aim of producing cheap food, has been another dangerous illusion. Healthy food cannot be produced cheaply. Crowded conditions increase diseases. Hormones and antibiotics used to increase growth, pollute the environment and affect consumers. They weaken the resistance of the animals which are then vulnerable to new viruses. Intensive farming is thought to be a major cause of pandemics in people. Viruses jump from wild populations to domesticated ones and then to their human contacts. Avian flu has been the most common, thought to be spread from intensive chicken rearing.

Food processing is also relevant. The huge international industry of fast and processed food uses countless additives to increase shelf life and make products more enticing. It is all aimed at adding value to natural products. Fatty and sweet fast foods have led to increasing obesity, which damages individual lives and is a significant burden on the NHS.

Years ago, a nutritionist commented that in the past parents did not need to worry about their children's eating habits. They might not eat enough of some important foods for a while, but would soon make up for it. Since then food had become so adulterated by synthetic chemicals that trick the taste buds, children (and adults) can no longer be trusted to eat healthily.

The horsemeat scandal provided one example of our failed system of food processing aimed at producing cheap food. Felicity Lawrence reported how very long supply chains across many countries enabled a few key players to buy the cheapest ingredients.

Deregulation in the UK and a dramatic cut in numbers of inspectors from 1700 at the time of the BSE crisis to 800 in 2013, allowed criminal adulteration to go uncontested. She identified a staggering 450 potentially vulnerable points in the chains of processing a variety of meat products. Enforcement in the industry had largely fallen to individual local authorities and their trading standards officers, and their budgets, too, had been slashed.

It seems every aspect of modern food production has reduced the quality of the food and increased pollution and carbon emissions.

Chapter 11   Austerity – a further step in privatisation

The banking crash in 2008 should have alerted people to the dangers of unregulated banking.   Two former Chancellors of the Exchequer admitted that the deregulation of the banks in the big bang had been the cause.

Instead the crash was seized as the perfect opportunity to encourage large scale privatisation. Austerity, a programme of cutting services and benefits was bound to shrink the economy, yet it was sold to the public as the only way to get the economy going again. The most credible explanation, and one that fits with neoliberal ideology, is that it was deliberately chosen to destroy state services in order to enable big business to come to the rescue and supply all our needs – privatisation.

The crash was claimed at the time to be caused by failed mortgages – in other words it was the fault of the poor. This fitted with the slogan of 'living within one's means' that was used to promote the policy However, a talk in Cromer by a former global banker, Andrew Rising, painted a very different picture. The crash was the direct outcome of deregulated banking procedures.

The trouble had started years earlier in America when the Glass-Stegall system, which had controlled the banks since the depression, was removed. This allowed the gambling side of banking to pair up with the investment and saving side.   It allowed currencies to be traded everywhere all the time and coincided, in Britain, with a venture into the 'knowledge' economy and the collapse of our manufacturing sector.

Bank trading developed into the 'derivatives' market.   Banks traded between themselves, borrowing money against good debts to allow expansion in a series of packages. After 10 to 15 years of trading no one knew who had what. Prices had increased with the costs of packaging and commissions, as well as inflation, but this didn't reflect any real production on the ground. The panic started in 2007 when a small think tank in America estimated the value of the 'derivatives' market at $1.4 quadrillion. This was about 40 times more than the world's output. The panic involved the whole banking sector. The value of derivates dropped dramatically by $400 trillion, because 'value' in banking is tied to 'confidence'. It is this largely illusory debt that people have had to pay back through very real austerity measures, while the banks were bailed out.

Austerity came at a crucial time for big business. Their continuing expansion and cut-throat competition meant that markets were saturated. They were desperate to expand in different ways. What could be safer than taking over services paid for by taxpayers or taking over food production, something needed every day? It was also an obvious good for investors and those hoping to work in corporations at some stage. A clear case of jobs for the boys.

It had short term advantages for lazy governments. It allowed them to appear to 'balance the books' by avoiding the immediate expenses of infrastructure - such as hospitals and railways. But only because they were not concerned about inevitably higher costs in the future.

Being at arm's length from service provision also cushioned the government from 'blame'. When things went wrong, they could be on the side of the public, equally shocked and demanding reform and compensation from the companies involved.

Choosing 'austerity' went against the independent economic advice from Lord Sterne, commissioned by the previous government. He advocated the traditional, tried and tested Keynesian system of government investment. In particular, investment in renewables and a greener infrastructure to revive the economy while countering that other major threat - climate change.

It went against professional advice from all the services affected, teachers, doctors and nurses, police and prison staff, the justice system, social services and local government.

I suggest that only an already degraded political debate controlled by sound bites, a complicit media, and a weak, divided and unimaginative opposition allowed this to happen. The simplistic domestic slogan of 'living within your income' was used to promote it and it was predicted to work within a few years. It utterly failed to do so.

But, sadly, it was extremely successful in promoting its real aim of shrinking the state - or undermining democracy - through privatisation. And, as it appeared and was claimed to succeed at the start, austerity become an acceptable economic policy to correct debt in many other countries as well.

Over time the widespread opposition has been proved correct. The dire predictions of so many professional people have been confirmed by daily reports through the years of dangerous failures in essential services. By 2018, with more cuts still to come, 'austerity' had succeeded in wrecking most of the services needed for a civilised country, even the background administrative services such as pension providers, the Charity Commission and the Land Registry. Productivity was at an all time low.

The system of law and order, the basis of stability in this country and something the Conservative Party has always prided itself on, provides just one example. Austerity cuts decimated many aspects of the system: cuts of over 1 billion, 40%, the deepest to any department by 2018. So much so that lawyers questioned the survival of our legal system and in 2019 barristers threatened to strike.

Legal aid was cut dramatically as were the wages of lawyers representing them, denying poorer people the basic right of equal representation.

The situation allowed one side to have representation, the other not. In some cases people tried to represent themselves despite not understanding court procedure. In family courts victims could be questioned by their abusers. The situation was so obviously damaging that in 2019 a criminal investigation was launched against the MOJ over suppressing internal research into the damage caused by people having to defend themselves.

Other aspects of the systems were equally badly damaged. Cuts to police numbers undermined their ability to enforce the law or help to prevent trouble.

Overcrowded prisons lacking facilities and activities became dangerous places for inmates and staff, with deaths in custody, suicides, riots and increased drug use. Some dangers to prisoners came directly from abusive staff conduct. Staff shortages led to gross unfairness when prisoners had to stay beyond their sentence because assessing them has become impossible.

Privatisation proved no answer. Criminal behaviour, corruption and undue force were and are present in private prisons and Youth Secure Training Centres as well as those run by the MOJ.

Privatising 70% of the probation service in 2015, with only high risk cases kept for the National Service, also proved a failure. It produced no savings and led to a 50% increase in serious crimes committed while on parole. In the private sector commercial interests dominated. The risk offenders posed to society was downplayed to meet government targets and unrealistically high workloads led to sentence plans sometimes being completed without meeting the offender.

Similarly, the privatisation of the forensic science service and serious cuts to its funding lowered standards with resulting injustice and the collapse of trials. Putting it under the control of the police compromised professional standards. Professor Gil quoted in the Independent as long ago as 2015 "..you're put under a lot of pressure to report what the police want you to report. .. If you're not protected from that,.. the more vulnerable forensic scientists are going to report cases wrongly. I'm absolutely convinced this is happening now."

At the same time cutting benefits increased inequality, poverty and deprivation. Its rhetoric increased social division, disrespect, intimidation and hate crime. Combined with low wages and the high costs of housing, heating, and transport, essential workers, even well qualified teachers and nurses who had invested in training, were branded 'scroungers'. They needed benefits to top up their wages. The benefit system which subsidised wages was ostensibly to help people, but in fact it benefited businesses. They could get away with paying unrealistically low wages. Tax payers were forced to make up the difference.

To this day (2020/21) the deterioration has continued across all our services, with countless reports in newspapers such as the Guardian of failings in policing, the justice system, dangerous prisons, cash strapped schools, increased poverty, increased homelessness, the need for foodbanks, the failure to protect women, children or the vulnerable. Failings in the Health Service have been dramatically revealed by the Covid19 pandemic.

The many scandals of the treatment of the Windrush generation and EU citizens are probably equally due to the Home Office's racist attitude as to the private companies carrying out the work.

Through neoliberal policies, first developed in American and readily adopted by the UK, capitalism has developed into the more extreme Selfish Capitalism. You may well ask, 'What sort of people could possible promote such damaging policies?' Oliver James, a psychologist who has treated many very wealthy but unhappy people, points to the close connection between neoliberalism and a personality disorder, 'Affluenza'. This is best described as an infectious   obsession with personal wealth and power.

Those afflicted define their lives through earnings, possessions, appearances and celebrity. Critically, they are incapable of empathy for others, so fail to value or protect fundamental needs; the need for emotional and material security; the need to feel in control our lives and to be able to express our feelings and thoughts. They disregard the importance of friendship and being part of a community. They are also never satisfied, always needing more. Wealth does not bring personal contentment. They are generally suspicious and paranoid, thinking the worst of others and unable to co-operate.

His claim that affluenza now affects the attitudes and behaviour of many of those in power, seems all too accurate when we look at the behaviour of leaders in many countries, including our own. In future we should take note of his insight when considering who is fit to be an MP.

My theory as to how affluenza develops makes use of the theory of 'cognitive dissonance'. This suggests that conflicting attitudes, beliefs or behaviours, produce a feeling of mental discomfort (dissonance) which lead people to change their views or behaviour in some way to reduce their internal discomfort. I am assuming that we all have a basic, I suspect innate, understanding of 'fairness' and a wish to act fairly ourselves. I am also assuming that people with privileges enjoy them and do not want to lose them. Quite young children provide clear examples. They are incensed and often articulate about any unfairness, but I have not heard any child complain about treats in their lives.

Cognitive dissonance poses a predicament for any of us benefiting from an unfair system. We feel uncomfortable. The best way to defeat our internal conflict is to blame the victim; to assume he suffers as a result of his own inadequacy. And we prosper because of our own efforts. We deserve our privileges.

The power of cognitive dissonance to control and change attitudes should not be underestimated. It is a classic brainwashing technique. We should consider the possibility that many of us, and particularly the elite, are brainwashed.

Whatever the process, Selfish Capitalism has institutionalised miserliness which drives policy in the UK for the benefit of the few, at the cost of democracy, the quality of life for most of us, even our safety.

Chapter 12 The False Myths and Tactics used to Promote Neo-liberal Policies

It is important to realise that neoliberal policies have been promoted by gross misrepresentation - smoke and mirrors. The role of advertising has been key. Years of psychological research had developed techniques to control and alter people's attitudes and desires. Slogans and lies were used to manipulate. Terms such as 'efficiency', 'sovereignty', 'sustainable' and 'defence' are among many misused to sell policies.

'Efficiency' which should refer to the good use of time, money and resources and a lack of waste to achieve a successful outcome, is often used to sell policies or actions which are cheaper or quicker – regardless of the use of resources or the outcome.

'Sustainability', which refers to actions which do not undermine the future by the careful use of resources has morphed into nearly the opposite, economically sustainable or in other words – profitable.

'Sovereignty' which should refer to our ability to rule ourselves has been hijacked by the far right to oppose cooperation with international groups unless for so called defence. The same group favour the power of corporations above national governments, and the power of central government over the public.

'Defence' is consistently misused to describe attack.

The dominant myth of neoliberal policies was that market forces could be relied on to provide what people needed. An unusual view. Traditionally, markets have been used to trade extra production. It had not been expected to supply basic needs. The current horror of market forces in action means that peasant farmers who grow the food for everyone else are often unable to afford to buy it for themselves.
In reality the myth was, and continues to be, a complete lie.

Market forces have never been used. There is no fair playing field. If there had been, nuclear power would have been stopped immediately, and the shortage of nurses would have led to higher pay. Any favoured industry was and is supported with grants and tax breaks. In many cases state assets were stripped - sold off cheaply - to benefit privatization. Another tactic used with pharmaceutical companies was to grant patents on pills largely developed by taxpayers' and charities' funding.

A telling example is the defence industry. Earlier governments had recognised armaments as a cost to the economy, albeit a necessary one. In contrast, in this privatising age, BAE, a global corporation, is treated as our national defence system, and lauded as a major asset. One of our remaining industries, it is promoted by royalty no less.

Mark Thomas in 'As Used on the Famous Nelson Mandela', analysed the costs, morality and efficiency of the arms trade. He found that arms remain a substantial cost to our economy, even when not including nuclear weapons. As far back as 2006, he estimated every conventional defence related job cost the taxpayer £13,106.30. He took several factors into account; direct subsidies, many types of government promotion and the cheap insurance for any bad debts provided by taxpayers through ECGD (Export Credit Guarantee Department).

A report for the Campaign Against the Arms Trade (CAAT) in 2016 using information from the Stockholm International Peace Research Institute shows that this remains the case. It estimates that direct subsidies for arms exports were about £104-£142 million in 2017 and they may be about £10 million more by now.

These arise from the same processes identified by Mark Thomas - export promotion via the Defence & Security Organisation (now Defence & Security Exports); the Defence Assistance Fund; the military attaché network, and official visits; and export credit guarantees which act as subsidised insurance against default.   It also identifies many mechanisms to provide indirect support: such as government / taxpayers funding of Research & Development; government/taxpayer absorption of most of the risk of cost overruns on major programmes.

In another policy area, a chilling example tells how corporations, by abusing market forces, have not only dominated the market, but also gained control of many of our global institutions. Through these they are able to direct national and global policy. The Corbett Report 'How and Why Big Oil Conquered the World' (2017) describes how oil companies in America first used a series of dirty tricks and secret deals to eliminate competition and gain dominance of the market and from that extraordinary wealth.

Then they used their wealth in a variety of ways to covertly influence governments, rulers and banking. By donating notionally altruistic foundations, the oil barons managed to influence education. They rewrote history and the teaching on medicines and farming practices to use their products, which further increased their wealth. Weapons and fuel became the basis for medicines and food production. Methane morphed into chemotherapy; nerve gases into pesticides, the nitrogen in explosives into fertilizer.

Traditional (benign) herbal medicines and farming practices were ousted and derided. This report echoes the claims of Vandana Shiva that the 'green revolution' in agriculture and modern medicine uses the tools of death and destruction.

Equally significant, the oil barons used their wealth to gain influence if not control in the UN, the IPPC and in other environmental organisations such as the World Wildlife Fund. After decades during which their scientists denied the warming effects of fossil fuels, they became directly involved in notionally addressing climate change and environmental conservation. There is no reason why they should not have done so. As it became all too obvious that the days of fossil fuels were numbered, it made sense for the oil barons to earn from the clean up and from developing benign alternatives. They were is a position to do so. However, the evidence in the report is that they have repeatedly skewed the debate to hamper action.

One early aspect of this was promoting the idea that population increase was the main cause of global warming, rather than industry and fossil fuels. An inaccurate analysis, as while the world's population has increased 2 times, the economy, the carbon footprint, has increased 6 times. And of course, this increase is in the west. Blaming large families in the third world, as happened, is 'blaming the victim'.

The report suggests that this view reflected the elitist ideas of eugenics, known to be held by some oligarchs. Whatever the reason, it took the pressure off attempts to reform energy policy, question capitalism and look for more civilised solutions. I remember the arguments in the 80s when those opposed to forced population control pointed out that poor families in the South had lots of children as they were needed to provide security in old age. The best way to stop this was to provide services common in the rich West; care in old age, education and voluntary methods of contraception. Kerala in India with exactly these policies provided a successful example.

In the democratic west, the idea that having more than two children is irresponsible fits with this view as does the policy of only supporting two children with child benefit. Larger families are penalised in the UK.

The linked stress on individual choices – each one of us making our global footprint smaller, was another way to divert attention from the need for total system change at government level. It is doubtless true that we will all have to change, but in too many ways we are helpless to make the relevant changes. We cannot avoid the packaging large companies use and finding organic produce is often hard as is avoiding products containing palm oil. People trying to live sustainably are hampered and demoralised.

An example of elitist thinking in global conservation bodies comes from the cruelty and contempt shown to native peoples by the 'debt-for-nature' swaps. In this Third World countries got debt relief only by giving up some of their land for environmental development projects. The contractors earned from managing the investments, but the locals, such as the aborigines of Palawan Island, were kicked off their land.

Several other policies have allowed business as usual to continue, such as carbon trading instead of a straightforward carbon tax. Carbon trading allows corporations not only to continue as usual and but also to earn from managing transactions. A more recent case is the huge publicity campaign to promote hydrogen as a green alternative, which will allow gas companies to continue production at great expense while it is very unlikely to cut carbon.

Most significant, right at the centre of the global effort to cut carbon, the Intergovernmental Panel on Climate Change (IPCC) does not and cannot produce meaningful and accurate reports. It has been handicapped by its terms of reference, set by Maurice Strong, an oil man with close links to the Rockefellers.

The IPCC is only allowed to consider the human causes of climate change. It offers no way of identifying the proportion human behaviour causes among other factors. As a result, the reports have been less convincing. They have encouraged those who do not believe human action is the main cause of climate change.

Worse, according to the Corbett Report, the terms of reference have made it impossible for accurate reports even on the result of human activity. The panel of 2,500 is split into three working groups. Group 1 writes the science reports. This has to be accepted by the other groups. But the Summary for Policymakers is written by a completely separate group independent of the science report. The Summary for Policymaker goes to the media, and the science report then has to agree with it. So the IPCC reports, which claim to come from top scientists are in fact political reports. No wonder many claim the figures for global warming have been vastly underestimated.

This report shows the almost unimaginable scale of control that a few corporation chiefs have on all our lives. Complaints about the revolving door between MPs and corporations, and the power of lobbying, pale into insignificance when compared to the control of global institutions. Can any country call itself democratic when global governance is so compromised?   (Most of the report concentrates on American firms, but it makes clear that European and other oligarchs have behaved in similar ways.)

There have been many other myths and slogans to confuse us. Indeed, I find it hard to identify any major policy not supported by false claims. Privatisation, for example, was promoted with the slogan 'private good, public bad'. An illusion. The problems of privatisation are legion.

Borrowing by banks is more expensive than by government, so funding privatised services is bound to cost more, quite apart from the profits paid to the private sector. No small matter given the obscenely inflated bonuses and wages paid.

Everything about privatisation is opposed to the culture of public service and democratic accountability. Their legal requirement is to make profits for shareholders, not to provide the best service. Creaming off profits from services is bound to make them more expensive. If, in the bidding war they are cheaper, and will therefore be claimed 'more efficient', this almost certainly implies a poorer service.   Splitting up services into several different private packages which is common, loses over all vison and control, all cohesion.

Commercial   confidentiality   destroys   accountability.   Competition between rival companies encourages problems to be denied and covered-up. Contracts fix policies for years allowing less flexibility at a time when technologies and needs are changing fast. Legal wrangles add to the cost. Finally, businesses can fail, and many have, leaving the tax payer to cover the costs.

Equally important, when a government is no longer in charge, it soon loses knowledge and becomes dependent on the private sector, whatever the cost.

The lie about the increased efficiency of privatisation has been exposed in a series of scandals in nearly every service. Indeed privatisation, working with the equally ideological 'austerity' programme has succeeded in destroying public services, ruining the economy and undermining democracy.

Of course, it was almost certainly true that public services were failing in many ways. That was a problem caused by bad or lazy government to be sorted out by them, with proper investment and forethought. There is nothing intrinsically different about the people working in both sectors. They have the same talents and the same weaknesses. It is up to government to design their own systems to allow talents to flourish and discourage laziness and greed.

Chapter 13   Brexit – the next mistake

Brexit fits well into the picture of leaders infected with affluenza; dominated by neo-liberal ideology, suspicious of others, unable to co-operate, or seek informed advice to make logical decisions.   A continuation of character traits evident among some Tory MPs ever since Thatcher's time which has inevitably led to increasingly miserable policies.

Brexit was a disaster for this country and an immoral imposition on the EU. It is impossible to know whether it was the fruit of incompetence and a frivolous attitude to government or a deliberate part of the same policy as 'austerity', aiming to give more power to corporations.

Was David Cameron completely out of touch with reality when he called an unnecessary referendum? Can we even assume he wanted a 'Yes' vote given his own hostility to Europe?

Was it just carelessness to give no thought to the difference between a first-past-the-post voting system which had given him a majority with only 24% of the vote, and a referendum in which 'every vote counted'?

Was he unaware of the hostility 'austerity' had caused, and so sure of his ability to control the situation that he allowed a party political matter to dominate policy?

Similarly, was it just carelessness that led to no plans for a possible 'No' vote? With no thought about the immense complications and expense of leaving, given how closely interwoven UK and European businesses were? Or about the complicated rights of EU citizens living here or British citizens living in the EU; or about Ireland and Scotland? Was he unaware how precious holidays on the continent were for countless people? With not even a decision as to how large a majority would be needed to change the status quo.

The remain campaign had little credibility as Cameron himself had been so critical of the EU. His MEP's had frequently voted against EU policies and the government failed to make use of the help or controls the EU offered. Over time the government had failed to inform the public about EU institutions, how they worked and the contributions they made to our society. It had failed to explain how interwoven our industry and other institutions were with EU companies. Relying on the slogan that 'No' meant 'a leap in the dark' was wholly inadequate, particularly in the context of years of drip feed hostility to the EU.

Detailing the problems would have been needed to expose the lies of the 'No' campaign, which relied largely on false promises and UKIP's inaccurate vilification of migrants and the EU. Migrants were the scapegoats for widespread failures in government policy in housing, schools, the NHS and low wages. Their vital contributions to society and the economy were ignored. No one put the record straight.

At the time I wondered if a deliberate distraction may have been part of Cameron's motive, given the distress caused by his cruel handling of desperate refugees. If so, in that aim at least, he was successful. Wanting a break with Europe was clearly in line with one wing of the party, Tories who were UKIP in all but name, so all the mismanagement may have been deliberate.

The design of the referendum could hardly have been bettered if a 'No' result had been the aim. 16 and 17 year olds and UK citizens living in Europe were excluded, while Commonwealth citizens living here could take part; and only a simple majority needed.

Whatever the motive, the timing of the referendum was criminally irresponsible. In the middle of global crises - war, the huge problems of refugees, climate change, nuclear threats and the financial crisis - the referendum was a destructive distraction for everyone. Even had the result been to stay in Europe, months of uncertainty was the last thing needed. As it is we and the EU are now condemned to spend countless years wasting time, energy and money on this ridiculous project instead of dealing with real problems. No politician of any moral standing would have imposed their party political agenda on this country and on the whole of Europe in such circumstances. The timing alone proves the Tory party unfit for government.

The campaign exemplified all that is worst in British attitudes and behaviour, egged on by misinformation, false myths and racist and jingoistic slogans.

The pivotal roles of the EU, its raison d''etre, were completely ignored. These were, firstly, the all important task of preventing wars in Europe. Replacing competitive nationalism with international co-operation on shared goals. Perhaps the continental European countries were more committed to this goal. They had suffered even more than us in wars as their lands were occupied and fought over.

The second major role was that of setting higher standards of welfare for workers, human rights and the environment in the global market place in contrast to those of China and the US. I attended a series of lectures in Cambridge (recorded in Spring in Winter) which made it clear that countries with weaker governance were depending on the EU to impose standards on them through trading rules. The UK itself benefited. We were known as the dirty man of Europe.

Instead, in the campaign, the EU was characterised as imposing government on us. Quite untrue when the rules needed for fair trading and super national issues such as pollution, were jointly agreed and other aspects of government were untouched. As is shown by the different policies on schooling, prisons, housing, defence, etc followed by each EU country.

The EU, with a more representative voting system was portrayed as undemocratic. The EU parliament was confused with its civil service. Many of us who wanted to remain were also critical of the EU for its lack of democracy. We wanted reform so that issues were considered by the parliament while being developed, rather than just in a final take-it-or-leave-it vote. But we could also make the same complaint about government here, that so called 'consultations' were over controlled and biased - frequently mere white washing. And that unelected quangos controlled much of national policy.

A great deal was made of the need for 'Sovereignty', control of our own laws. 'Sovereignty' sounds so good. Being independent, running ourselves as we choose and standing on our own feet. But it was a bit late in the day to want isolation. It flew in the face of our colonial history, where, as the mother country we had links to countless others and benefited from their work and resources. As one immigrant remarked ' We only came here because you came to us first.'

It is also deeply ironic to laud sovereignty in todays' world because it has largely been ceded deliberately to the market and the banks. Privatisation and globalisation are the biggest threats to sovereignty. When UK firms take on services, parliament's sovereignty is diminished. When foreign firms are involved, as is often true, the sovereignty of the country is at stake.

It was also ironic that defence – traditionally absolutely concerned with sovereignty – was omitted from consideration. Membership of NATO destroys our ability to control our armed forces. UKIP was happy to have our troops die in the defence of other European countries and Turkey. Absurdly, the 'No' campaign promised money for the NHS and no serious problems with the economy for an easy deal was certain.

I found the two saddest mistakes were the idea that getting out of Europe would protect us from globalisation and protect our fishing rights. Globalisation has been the child of the US and the UK. We had infected European governments with our neoliberal ideas. Getting out of Europe would make us more dependent on the most ruthless global companies as we would risk losing the protection of European values. Similarly, it was our own government that sold fishing rights to large corporations – their friends. Although claiming to be the party for businesses, they have never been interested in supporting small fisheries or any other small businesses. Indeed it is difficult to think of any small business or individual who could benefit from damaging trade with our nearest and largest customers, and making work in and travel across Europe more difficult.

The vicious language of the campaign legitimised intolerance and hate. Lying and misinformation became the norm and has continued in the aftermath. Hate crimes and extreme threats increased. Jo Cox was murdered. The conduct of social affairs was degraded by the Brexit campaign.

It can be no surprise that such a destructive campaign had an appalling result.   The situation continued to deteriorate. Theresa May immediately changed the terms of Brexit. Controlling migration became the sole focus. It fitted her personal priority, shown by her term as Home Secretary, but was disguised as the will of the people. Funding the NHS was abandoned within a few days, followed by a determination to reduce the sovereignty of parliament. She worked to stop debate and decisions. A successful economic agreement with the EU seemed of no importance.

Her bossy and rigid style, exemplified by the meaningless slogan 'Brexit means Brexit' left EU politicians bewildered. She seemed the very worst person to negotiate anything, yet continued to be described in the media as the only wise choice. During 2018, her snap election misfired and she only survived with support from the Ulster Unionists. With the continuing chaos in her cabinet and as increasing evidence of the costs and uncertainty of Brexit emerged, at last a few questions were asked, but there was no noticeable change.

Although the referendum did not have legal force, any questions as to its power to change policy were immediately drowned out as being 'undemocratic' – irrespective of the lies and suspected illegal funding on which the choice was made. Later the call for a second referendum as more facts emerged, met with the same fate. It seemed obvious to me that the Leave group knew they had won by a trick and would fail a second attempt. Indeed, an LSE (London School of Economics) analysis of the figures of those who did not or could not vote has shown that the majority was in favour of Remain at the time of the referendum and has remained so in subsequent polls.

Blame for the deadlock in parliament must be shared by other parties. Co-operation seemed impossible. The Labour party in particular was split on whether to support remain or leave. Failure to act together at this point led to May's resignation and Boris Johnson's selection by Tory party members and soon after to Boris Johnson's triumph – a big majority in 2019, which demonstrated our failing democracy.

The whole point of a functioning democracy is that it allows the electorate to vote out parties who do them harm. The Tory party, of which Boris had been an important member, had imposed austerity and privatisation, which devastated most of the institutions we rely on for a decent standard of living. The evidence was clear. Public discontent was widespread. In addition, the impasse over Brexit called into question the government's competence. And for a significant minority the climate and ecological crises were priorities demanding immediate attention and very different policies.

Yet none of this had enough effect. The Tories got more votes than any other party, 43%, (although admittedly not a majority in the country). These people voted for more of the same and to continue with Brexit.

A case of turkeys voting for Christmas. It was as if they had been mesmerised by the slogan "Get Brexit Done" in the hope that this would allow attention to the 'real' problems they claimed to care about. Yet two minutes thought, as a few commentators acknowledged at the time, showed that 'getting Brexit done' was a fallacy. It would inevitably lead to years more negotiation. Money and time would have to be spent on leaving and other trade talks instead of on the NHS and other crucial services it was claimed the majority wanted. The only logical way to get Brexit done was to cancel it.

Many factors must have influenced this vote. A failed opposition, with Labour's long internal quarrels, the split between remainers and leavers leading to equivocation over Brexit; a general distrust of the Lib Dem's following their time in coalition; anger with all politicians over the impasse in Parliament; and the rigged voting system restricting influence to a few marginal seats, so that huge resources could be piled into these areas to influence views.

But it seems clear, too many of the electorate, although a minority in the country, confirmed the deep malaise in our political life. A politically under educated public, for whom lies have become acceptable, evidence and the truth irrelevant and slogans win the day.

It is important to realise the role of our unfair voting system. The support of 43% of the voters gave Johnson an 88 seat majority in Parliament, but represented a minority of the voters. The combined votes of 'remain' supporting parties was greater. They failed to register because the opposition was split into many different parties, and our voting system only caters for 2 parties. When non-voters were taken into account, nearly a third of the electorate, then Johnson's support drops to only 29%.

The political situation in the UK at this time of crises in 2019 was nothing short of a disaster. We had a government whose policies have undermined all our services, increased inequality and poverty and distress, and promoted the pollution and habitat destruction which threatens life on earth, while also continuing with expensive and dangerous so called 'defence' systems. Yet it seems there was little chance of getting rid of them for several years to come.

Chapter 13   Foreign policy

The problems suffered by the domestic population as a result of government policies is nothing compared to the horror experienced by others abroad, in part caused by our 'defence' policy and our choice of allies.

'Defence' has long been accepted as an essential, moral and legal responsibility of government which has to be paid for by taxes. But I think most people imagine this as defending our land from invasion, self defence, which is many miles away from what happens now. Our misnamed defence policy is offensive, immoral and deadly. A system dominated by delusions of grandeur, the need for global status, the interests of global corporations and the interests and mind set of the arms industry, where killing is the only option.

Arms production, our misnamed 'defence system', has changed completely. Nowadays, attack has become our 'defence system'. While still a major cost to our economy, heavily subsidised by taxpayers, the interests and profits of the arms industry, BAE, have come to dominate government policy. BAE looks always for new ingenious and more powerful methods of killing and new threats, in its quest for continual expansion. The government lauds arms sales as good business for the country, whereas in fact they are a cost to taxpayers. Government are in fact working for BAE's profits.

Armed intervention has become the first and often only option in confronting perceived problems in other countries, however absurd and cruel. When David Cameron in 2015 claimed to be moved by the sight of Alan Kurdi's drowned body, the response of the UK, lauded by Cameron, was to increase the bombing of Syria. What led him to this incoherent and cruel conclusion? How exactly could more bombing stop refugees trying to escape, when it was the bombs and other persecutions that were causing them to flee in the first place?

The aftermath of destruction is of no interest to the arms industry, which explains the lack of planning by our government to restore countries we have helped to devastate.

Our 'ethical defence policy' has meant nothing. The government have actively promoted supplies to repressive regimes and areas of conflict. Mark Thomas in 2006 exposed the scandal of bribery, corruption, criminality, loopholes and very lax controls, which allow gun runners to export guns and instruments of torture almost anywhere. The government gives priority to arms sales whatever the horror and instability that might cause.

The result is a world awash with arms - In 2006, an estimated 640 million guns, with one person killed every minute, half a million killed each year, and 60% ending up in the hands of criminals and rebel groups. Armaments have a long lifetime. With an estimated 8 million being added each year, the total must now be considerably higher.

We have joined with others, our allies or NATO, in disastrous, ill-planned attacks on other lands in support of business interests, or political ideology, all claimed as 'defence'. As Jeremy Corbyn continues to stress – whatever the problems in other countries, and there are many, war is no solution. Instead, these wars have caused immense destruction, death, and suffering and destabilised large areas of the globe. They add to the suffering already caused by colonialization, exploitation by large corporations and climate change. There is no end in sight to these tragedies as other states and interest groups rush in to pursue their own commercial, religious and political interests in the power vacuum caused by our general ignorance of other societies and lack of planning.

The ghastly ongoing tragedies of Syria, Libya and the Yemen are just three terrible examples of a failed 'defence' policy. They are a major factor in recruiting 'terrorists', which has made our citizens a target, both abroad and at home. Thousands of protestors, myself included, warned Blair's government this would happen before the Iraq war. The hate and frustration caused by decades of bullying and subjection was bound eventually to spill over into guerrilla attacks and religious extremism.

An expanding NATO has increased tensions in the world. When it started the NATO alliance represented the West's fear of Russia and communism. Russia's fear was similarly represented by the Warsaw Pact alliance. After the fall of the Berlin Wall, the breakup of the USSR and the apparent demise of communism, NATO represented the triumph of the free market system and democracy over communism. It expanded its remit to combat other ideologies seen as undemocratic or illiberal. NATO has been involved in disastrous interventions in the Middle East and Afghanistan.

By promoting the advantages of 'democracy' and the free market, 14 former Warsaw pact countries on or near the borders of Russia were persuaded to join NATO. Western arms now surround a significant part of Russia's border. In its weakened state, Russia lost its buffer zone. Putin may be rightly accused of paranoia and aggression, but how could he not feel threatened?

We have failed to learn the basic lesson that a good defence policy must not threaten others. For us to be safe others must be safe and crucially, feel safe. It is no good saying the missiles near Russia are merely for defence, if they are perceived as threatening. Like bullies everywhere, we have failed to listen to, or believe, other points of view. The result, war in Ukraine, intervention in Syria, an arms race with tragically wasted resources, deteriorating economies and increasing tension. We should be asking ourselves how much responsibility we share for the success of Putin?

Absolutely the worst aspect of our defence policy is the mis-named 'independent nuclear deterrent'. The horrors of Trident have been described already. It risks catastrophic destruction by accident at every moment. We know people go mad, we know computers malfunction. Several near accidents have already happened and they are getting more likely. There have been plenty of warning voices.

Over all, our defence policy is a major threat to our survival and global civilisation. It has been a tragic waste of resources which could have supported many forms of peace making.

Our choice of the US as our major ally, so important to our sense of special status and privilege, has also had a disastrous influence on our policies. We must face some facts about this ally.

The US was the first country to have deliberately used nuclear weapons for mass destruction. While often excused in terms of ending the war and saving allied lives, both bombs were dropped when Japan was known to be on its knees, only weeks from running out of fuel. It is more credible that nuclear weapons were used to pre-empt an imminent Russian invasion, which would have allowed them to claim victory in Japan. In other words, this was the start of the cold war against Russia. Another totally cynical reason was the wish to find out how well the bombs worked after all the money spent on their development. Hence one bomb of each type dropped on civilians in towns not previously attacked, so their full impact could be judged.

Since then, as a superpower the US has pursued what it sees as its own national interest, ruthlessly, either supporting US businesses, or defeating different political views. Over the years, its covert interference has destabilised countless other countries, destroying democratic governments, and leading to long term instability, violence and crime. Countries in South America have been a major target, but the Vietnam war also demonstrated a completely inaccurate analysis of the political situation by politicians who then lied deliberately to their own people. In both Cuba and Vietnam US actions drove those countries to become communist, further confirming US paranoia and obsession.

The US, although a major aggressor in the world, and with its own country suffering from violence, poverty, racism, pollution, social inequality and a poor health service, has assumed the role of policeman. And is apparently supported in this by its allies. It has used its power and wealth as a bully, attacking individuals, countries, and threatening international institutions. In its arrogance it invades a country without any knowledge of, or respect for, the social values and systems there, increasing global conflict, making new enemies. And all that before Trump! We must hope for better things with Joe Biden.

The idea of a 'war on terror', first used by George Bush as an excuse to attack Afghanistan, greatly increased the situations where attack is justified. Although many thought his real reason was to gain access to oil, crime became accepted as an excuse for war. In this case, ludicrously, the criminal activity of Saudi pilots was used as an excuse for war on a different country. Since then, strikes against supposed enemies in many countries have brought a huge increase in tension, death and destruction among civilians.

The use of drones has made the situation worse. Drones allow war to be carried out secretly and without danger to the aggressor. Their use undermines international law and blurs the distinction between war and 'policing', where there is no legitimacy for that policing. They are a gross violation of the privacy and security of populations, increasing tension, death and distress. They can only increase hatred and terrorism. Killing by drone, whether intentionally or by accident, is just as bad as any other murder committed on foreign soil. It is no better than the poison killings attributed to Russia, or the murder of the journalist in the Saudi embassy in Turkey.

Armed interventions of all sorts have been a major factor in destabilising the world, inflicting death and destruction, creating refugees. They have undermined international law and the importance of political solutions and peace making through diplomacy. It is not an exaggeration to say they have led to barbarism.

War is not the only destabilising feature. Alliances can be just as dangerous, especially when countries do not understand each other's societies, and when individuals or other countries' interests can manipulate the situation.

The film 'Bitter Lake' by Adam Curtis shows a disastrous series of unintended consequences stretching over decades, from American alliances with the kings of Afghanistan and Saudi Arabia, started by Roosevelt in 1946. These were to be of benefit to both sides, by enabling modernisation in Afghanistan while protecting oil supplies for the US. But in a series of events over time they have contributed to the destabilisation of the whole area.

To give just one example, the alliance with Saudi Arabia led to the US protecting Wahhabism, a radical and violent form of Islam. It hates everything to do with empires and wished to return to a way of life according to their interpretation of the basic Islamic texts. Their aim was, and still seems to be, to set up a worldwide caliphate. US support allowed this ideology to spread. It formed the basis of the West's enemies in the Mujahideen, Taliban, Al-Qaeda, and IS.

Another festering sore in the Middle East is the situation in Israel. The British government allowed the Jews to settle in Palestine just after the second World War, completely misjudging the consequences. So, we should take a major share of responsibility in helping to resolve the difficulties, yet have done less than nothing. Israel, a traumatised nation, has, in its turn, become the aggressor. Palestinians have suffered far too much, far too long. And we have favoured the aggressor, turning a blind eye to their abuses. Even talking to Palestinians, as Jeremy Corbyn has done, is considered traitorous. This unending tragic situation has inevitably increased hatred and ideas of revenge.

Chapter 15 The context for global political reform in 2020 - The climate emergency, the extinction of species and pandemics

(This chapter relies heavily on notes for a talk by David North at the Cley Nature Reserve in North Norfolk in 2020 which he kindly shared with me.)

Natural systems are in a state of crisis. The planet is warming. NASA has confirmed that the planet's average surface temperature has risen about 1.62 degrees Fahrenheit (0.9 degrees Celsius) since the late 19th century. Most of the warming has occurred in the past 35 years, with the six warmest years on record taking place since 2014.

This change is driven largely by increased carbon dioxide and other human-made emissions into the atmosphere. Figures from the Global Monitoring Laboratory at the Mauna Loa Observatory in Hawaii show an increase in Carbon Dioxide from just over 300 parts per million in the 1960s to an estimate of nearly 420 in 2020.

Life is thinning. Species are declining, their populations shrinking. Nature is under threat as never before. Species and habitats are being damaged everywhere we look. The Living Planet Index which monitors 10,000 representative populations of 3,000 species of mammals, birds, reptiles, amphibians and fish says global populations have declined by on average 60% over the last 50 years.

These two changes are linked and the reasons are clear. Human activity has destroyed the balance in nature in five ways - through the unsustainable use and over-exploitation of natural resources, through habitat loss, pollution, invasive alien species and human induced climate change. We have known about the impacts of CO_2 on the climate for over 100 years and have done nothing.

We need to understand that all of life is linked in one planetary system, the Gaia principle, first proposed by James Lovelock. Living organisms interact with their surroundings on Earth to form a self-regulating synergistic and complex system that helps to maintain and perpetuate the conditions for life on the planet.

(Synergy describes the situation when two or more system/organisms interact to produce greater benefits than the sum of benefits from each acting alone. It shows the helpful influence of co-operation.)

Homeostasis is the name given to the process of maintaining conditions to allow life. Many of us will have learnt about the magic of photosynthesis at school. It is one example of homeostasis, a process of maintaining a balance of elements in the air, and producing living matter. Plants use sunlight, carbon dioxide and water to produce sugars, and oxygen, maintaining a breathable air.

$$6 \, CO_2 + 6 \, H_2O \rightarrow C_6H_{12}O_6 + 6 \, O_2.$$

Without plants animals could not exist, as we cannot make food.

But maybe many of us do not realise that this same principle applies to all life systems, including our climate. The complex links between the terrestrial, marine and atmospheric systems are essential to maintain the conditions necessary for life on this planet to thrive.

Life exists in a thin layer around our planet which extends only 20 miles into our atmosphere and 20 miles under the ground. Biodiversity in this layer is the source of our air, our food, our health and the systems that support our lives. It includes the carbon, nitrogen and phosphorus cycles. The atmosphere contains highly reactive gases such as oxygen, methane and carbon-dioxide which are all by products of life.

The natural world is our home and our life-support system. We are part of nature. The last 10,000 years, the Holocene age, was a period of stability which allowed human civilisation to grow precisely because natural systems flourished. A combination of the Arctic summer sea ice, ice cover in Greenland, the great boreal forests of Canada and Russia, the tropical forest of the Amazon and healthy living seas together maintained a stable climate for us for the past 6,000 years. During this period global average temperatures varied by no more than 1 degree centigrade.

Today, in the Anthropocene age, the countless changes we have made, and continue to make, have disrupted the homeostatic balance of our living systems. Each change produces another, the domino effect.

Over the last 20 years the situation has got much worse. The human population has doubled, but economic activity, the capitalist economy, our carbon footprint, has increased six times. The scale of human activity is breath taking.

> *Globally human activities move more soil, rock and sediment each year than other natural processes combined*
>
> *Factories and farming remove more nitrogen from the atmosphere than all the Earth's natural processes*
>
> *Since the industrial revolution we have released 2.1 trillion metric tonnes of CO_2 into the atmosphere creating levels not seen for over 3 million years*
>
> *Today there are about 3 trillion trees on the planet, down from six trillion at the dawn of agriculture*
>
> *Farmland annually produces 4.8 billion head of livestock – we extract 80 million tonnes of fish from the oceans each year*
>
> *If you weighed all the mammals on the planet around 3% of the biomass is wild animals; the rest is us (30%) and our livestock (67%)*

Plastic is now global – every beach however remote contains granules of plastic as do most seabirds and fish. ('The Human Planet How we created the Anthropocene.' Lewis and Maslin)

The tragedy is that we have already passed limits beyond which the Earth as we, and our forebears, have known it for millennia will cease to be. We can't ever replace the melted glaciers, the complex tropical forests we have cleared, the species made extinct, the coral reefs that are dying or restore the seasons as they once were.

The threat is that, unless we act now and decisively, climate change will be unstoppable. This is because warming will be increased by 'feed back loops' we cannot control. For example, melting permafrost will release huge additional amounts of methane, melting ice will change ocean currents., a destroyed amazon forest will start contributing carbon dioxide instead of absorbing it. As far as I know, the worst case scenarios currently given do not cover the horrors this might lead too, nor the shortened timescale.

Chapter16 The devastating effect of capitalist development and political ideologies on people and societies.

The huge increase in knowledge, science and technology, together with political systems ostensibly dedicated to the rule of law and fairness, might be expected to produce rich and successful societies, a flowering of civilisation. Although a few 'have never had it so good', for the many this has proved a mirage. Capitalist activity has caused massive social problems and threatens bigger ones.

We are part of nature, so the pollution that is destroying other life forms is also harming us. Dangerous air pollution is causing early deaths all over the world, including the UK. Residues of pollution in food from factor farming and intensive agriculture affect our health. The adulteration of foods to make them more appetising may well be the cause of obesity. We have no idea yet whether or how much the plastic which is now endemic in soil and water may be affecting us.

In the developing world pollution is much worse, more widespread with devastating consequences. Oil, nuclear radiation and other dangerous substances have been allowed to destroy ecosystems and people's lives. Rich societies have failed to use regulations to counter pollution. 'The polluter pays' and 'The precautionary principle' have been ignored and Ecocide is not an international law. Corporations can pollute with impunity, their only legal requirement being to make profits. In the conflict between democratic values and capitalist greed, capitalism has dominated and still does. The result is widening inequality with very few super rich, one might say obscenely rich, many struggling to survive and far too many suffering poverty, starvation and other dangers.

Fiercer and increasingly frequent storms, floods, mudslides, and droughts are everywhere.

So far, at least until Covid19, the devastation caused by the capitalist exploitation of resources has impacted most severely on the third world. Despite countless reports and conferences detailing the threats, richer countries have continued to deny the scale and urgency. Action has fallen far short of what is needed. It remains to be seen whether Covid19 will change this. So far the signs are bad.

It is important to realise the scale of greed in capitalism and the control it exercises. The survival of peasant farming communities around the world is threatened not only by the changing climate and loss of wildlife, but also by the institutions and policies of 'democratic' Western countries -GATT (The General Agreement on Trade and Tariffs) and IPRs (Intellectual Property Rights). Deliberate policies.

Vandana Shiva describes the World Trade GATT treaty as the modern Papal Bull. The Papal 'Bull of Donation' at the time of Columbus gave all lands discovered within a large area to the Christian kings of Europe. It completely denied native populations any rights. Now, through the GATT treaty, TNCs are allowed to patent living organisms. As Vandana Shiva says, 'The colonies have been extended to interior spaces, the 'genetic codes' of life-forms, from microbes and plants to animals and humans'.

This is theft of the 'commons' on an unprecedented scale.
Free trade and liberalisation imposed by the West were supposed to end protectionism, but, mainly through IPRs, the West, particularly the US has invented a new form of protectionism which directly threatens the livelihoods of peasant farmers.

As peasant farmers produce most of the world's food anything threatens them threatens us all.

Not content with the power and riches gained over others by economic domination – the 'free' world, the 'democratic' West has dominated with old fashioned colonial style military force – often through NATO. The West is not the only villain. But Western governments must take a large share of the blame for the tragic results of countless attacks on other countries over the decades to overcome communism, or for oil, or to change a regime. These catastrophic wars of intervention always promoted cynically as 'defence' demonstrate the supreme arrogance and greed of western democratic countries and their total ignorance of other societies. It is no surprise that interventions have made matters worse.

After the ravages of both World Wars millions of people recognised the desperate need for strong global governance to regulate the behaviour of national governments and bring peace. The UN was set up with the best of intentions to take over from the League of Nations which had proved impotent.

In recognising the Universal Rights of Man, it clearly aimed for the good of all nations and all peoples. There are thirty one articles in the UN Declaration of Human Rights. The first 7 are copied below:

> *Article 1 All human beings are born free and equal in dignity and rights. They are endowed with reason and conscience and should act towards one another in a spirit of brotherhood.*
>
> *Article 2 Everyone is entitled to all the rights and freedoms set forth in this Declaration, without distinction of any kind, such as race, colour, sex, language, religion, political or other opinion, national or social origin, property, birth or other status. Furthermore, no distinction shall be made on the basis of the political, jurisdictional or international status of the country or territory.*

Article 3 Everyone has the right to life, liberty and security of person.

Article 4 No one shall be held in slavery or servitude; slavery and the slave trade shall be prohibited in all their forms

Article 5 No one shall be subjected to torture or to cruel, inhuman or degrading treatment or punishment.

Article 6 Everyone has the right to recognition everywhere as a person before the law.

Article 7 All are equal before the law and are entitled without any discrimination to equal protection of the law. All are entitled to equal protection against any discrimination in violation of this Declaration and against any incitement to such discrimination.

By its charter, the UN It was dedicated to work for international peace and security, international cooperation; protecting human rights, delivering humanitarian aid, promoting sustainable development, upholding international law. All the things we clearly need and all supporting democratic values.

However, some of the powerful did not wish for peace. The US, Britain and France, continued to pursue domination through a series of brutal wars against supposed communist regimes and colonies. The nuclear arms race and the cold war added another dimension.

Absolutely nothing good can be said about nuclear arms. There is no indication that this horrible threat brought people to their senses. The nuclear arms race has wasted huge resources in producing more and more terrible weapons, while attacks were justified to stop others gaining the bomb. The scale became so ludicrous that their use would be suicidal as well as genocidal. The threat of nuclear annihilation has been with us since soon after the end of the second world war. It is the fourth threat facing mankind right now, but has become so normal a part of global politics that it is rarely recognised as such by the rogue nuclear nations. Nuclear weapons are the least democratic weapon; controlled secretly by a few people relying on computers, who have the power to unleash devastation in seconds.

It is difficult to understand the mind set or morals of nations prepared to use the threat of annihilation as a means of power. MAD - Mutually Assured Destruction - is the only accurate description.

You would think that these nations would be outlawed as rogues, yet the tragedy is that they have been allowed to control and undermine the work of the UN. The nuclear powers, the most aggressive and power hungry nations, were given the controlling power of the veto as permanent members of the Security Council. Very soon the cold war between Russia and the US and its allies undermined the work of the UN. Power politics of the worst sort have continued to plague the UN despite the good work of its agencies.

As a result, International Law has been severely undermined. The failure of the nuclear nations to uphold the Non-Proliferation Treaty is one early significant example.

Since then, the good work done after the second world war to frame laws to protect civilians and make combatants keep to laws has been ignored by many countries. International Law depends on voluntary compliance and when ignored loses its power to civilise.

We are in a time of increasing barbarity in so many areas: The brutal conduct of war – using chemical weapons, starvation and rape against civilians, the hostile treatment of refugees, the trafficking and abuse of children, slavery, the lack of care for the vulnerable.

The situation got worse after 9/11 when crimes were seen as a legitimate excuse for war, even for war on a different country. The US and its allies assumed the role of global policemen, aided considerably by the use of drones. This is a nightmare situation - the arch bully as policeman. I cannot think of anything more likely to cause the hatred that drives terrorism than the triumphalist domination of Western Christian democracies over communist or Muslim countries.

Chapter 17   Three Principles for urgent global reform and some obvious roadblocks to it.

It is clear the old ways have failed disastrously and monumental system change is needed urgently.   The West in particular needs a total revolution in the way we live: how we travel, how we work, what we eat, our lifestyles, our priorities and how our economy works. Only then will we be able to deal with the many linked crises confronting the world. These must include not only global warming, species extinction, pandemics, nuclear devastation and economic collapse, but also the linked social disasters of extreme inequality, poverty and starvation in many countries, slavery, human trafficking, the persecution of minorities and individuals and the devastation of war.

New principles, aims and institutions must be developed to deal with the new situation. Change will not be easy. There are many roadblocks to reform, but it is possible. People are highly adaptable and inventive. Covid19 has shown how fast things can be changed when people and institutions co-operate. Thousands have been calling for decades for reforms to herald a kinder, fairer, safer world. There are countless solutions and many willing to do the work at every level of society. The tragedy is that those in power have delayed change so long, and been allowed to do so by their public.

The first principle addresses HOW we make the changes. It must be from the bottom up - grassroots inspired and controlled change. This is not a new idea. The UN Conference in Rio on Sustainable Development as long ago as 1992, stressed the importance of grass roots control for developing countries, because only people at the grass roots know what their priorities are and what resources they have.

In this new situation when competitive, exploitative capitalism has brought us all to the brink of disaster, we are all having to develop from scratch. It is also true that only when people will be directly affected by the choices they make that they think deeply about them beforehand and learn quickly from mistakes.

Critically also, Information from countless sources is needed to choose wisely because we have no idea what other's jobs or lives entail. Central control, whether in global institutions such as the World Bank, or national or local government, even those practicing 'representative' democracy, misses out on masses of relevant information. Leaders have their own narrow interests at heart and are ignorant about many aspects of society, particularly so in advanced, rapidly changing scientific and technological societies. Government is simply out of touch with reality. Incapable of making sensible choices.

A tiny example comes from my own research into 'consultation' about two Highways decisions in my area. I was surprised by the mass of varied but very relevant information that came from talking to many who would be affected. Information not once considered or even heard by the Council. They were equally astonished by the hostility to their plans for a bypass, which was overturned, as they had only talked to one small group.

There is plenty of evidence that grassroots self-help can be far more effective in emergencies. Mary Robinson gives many examples in her book 'Climate Justice' of communities solving problems with scarce resources, when larger institutions had failed.

Similarly, in the film 'The Accidental Anarchist' Carne Ross describes many situations where anarchy, self-government, by people is deep distress worked well. This has been confirmed by the behaviour of local communities during the Covid19 crisis. Local groups have been more effective than government diktat. It seems that 'normal' people often have more good sense than their leaders. At the very least, unlike central government, they are in touch with detailed day-to-day conditions, both the problems and the possibilities. They think small which is often the answer.

A grassroots approach implies many more people, a significant proportion of adults and older children, will be involved in a participatory democracy. They will use community groups, citizens assemblies and referanda to decide policies that can no longer be left to political parties. People must be supported so as to be able to spend the time and energy needed, which means other work should not be all consuming. Critically, whistle blowers, instead of being treated as troublemakers, will be highly valued.

Grassroots involvement demands transparency. People need to know the facts. Getting rid of the secrecy common in today's politics will be an essential step in reducing the endemic corruption and incompetence we suffer from.

While using grassroots' information and control in our own districts and countries, we must recognise that many problems are regional or global and need to be addressed at that level. To reconcile this with grassroots activity, 'subsidiarity' should be the principle of government. That is - making decisions at the most local level possible.

And, when global action is needed, it should also come from grassroots requests and its implementation should be in the hands of local people. We must not repeat the catastrophic corruption and exploitation of the capitalist world when large grants end up in rich people's bank accounts, or when the world bank demands changes to suit the rich countries' business interests rather than the social needs of developing countries.

Clearly many countries will not implement this principle. It will only be possible in nominally democratic states and, even in those, many governments will try to hold on to their ideologies and power. That should not stop us. Providing a successful model can only help.

The second principle addresses Capitalism. Capitalism as we know it must go. It is at the heart of our problems. It is killing us. The growth that it demands is unsustainable. The interest rates it demands are killing the economies of poorer countries as well as causing damaging inequality within countries.

We need a type of 'doughnut economy', working within the limits of the globe to supply the needs of all, including those of poorer countries. An economy which focuses on wellbeing not GDP and aims at a steady state economy, to provide the essentials for a good but modest life as efficiently as possible.

This implies being creative with the resources we already have – using and reusing them, mending and adapting them. Built in obsolescence must go. The throwaway culture and any ideas of 'retail therapy' for the rich must go. At the same time financial subsidies for dangerous industries must stop and taxes and regulations used to encourage benign and sustainable processes.

The central idea in Capitalism that only paid work is work, and only goods sold in a market have any value, must go. The new economy must recognise that crops grown for home consumption are just as valuable as any sold. And that caring for children or relatives at home is similarly valuable.

Another linked theme that must go is the practice of only undertaking work if there is a market. Recycling items, for example only happens if a profit can be made, whatever the damage storing the waste might cause. The aims of a new economy would be first to reduce waste – something capitalist societies claim to pursue, but have failed to do. Then to take responsibility for making waste harmless as a duty. The cost accepted as a social necessity.

In addition to Kate Raworth's 'Doughnut Economics', there are plenty of alternative suggestions for economic systems, including the fine example of Bhutan. Their king, as long ago as 1972, declared, "Gross National Happiness is more important than Gross Domestic Product."

His sustainable economic policy gives equal importance to non-economic (monetary) aspects of wellbeing. He established the 'Gross National Happiness Index', as a measurement for use across all policy areas, with increasing happiness as the aim. It covers nine different aspects of life - Psychological wellbeing, Health, Education, Time use, Cultural diversity and resilience, Good governance, Community vitality, Ecological diversity and resilience and Living standards.

The growth demanded by capitalism has been produced by unsustainable consumer spending driven by advertising. Advertising has been a major tool of capitalism. People need straightforward information about services and products. But advertising - the deliberate manipulation of views and wishes by psychological means, designed to drive excessive and often harmful consumerism - must go. Advertising always misleads. It usually portrays the opposite of reality. When, for example, has an advert for cars ever acknowledged traffic jams, queues, poisonous fumes and deadly accidents? How many banks, focused solely on profit, instead sell themselves as the friend in need?

I am one of those who think the practice of using advertising to pay for services must go, whether on the internet or in the press and media. And that this will bring a huge social benefit. A more peaceful world, leaving people free from the constant harassment of sales. It will unlock the tight control of businesses over our lives and our ideas.

We will, of course, then have to pay for those services directly. This might seem onerous, but I think, will bring benefits, too. Having to pay for emails, tweets, etc, will make people think twice before sending them. It should cut down on the current deluge of communications which reminds me of the geese in 'Animal Farm' who deliberately drowned out sensible ideas.

The power of advertising to influence political and social values should lessen significantly. Once people are involved in learning about situations and deciding policies themselves, they will be far less vulnerable to simplistic ideological slogans.

The basic unit of exchange, money, will remain essential, but the rules controlling it through capitalism must change. Working out an alternative to capitalism and money supply should not be beyond the wit of man. I am very ignorant, but am confident that others will find a way. All the rules about money were invented by people and have been deliberately set for the advantage of bankers, traders and investors. They are not natural laws. The rules must change to suit the situation.

It is clear that vast amounts of money will need to be invested to deal with the emergencies and change to a sustainable way of life. The monetary cost of policies should not be the deciding factor as is usual today. Instead social or environmental needs should dominate. Essential policies should never be turned down because they are 'too' expensive.

The very general illusion that money is automatically associated with power and knowledge should go. There is no evidence that rich people know more. Indeed at the personal level poorer people have to use much more intelligence and ingenuity to survive than those who can just throw money at any problem. Endowing institutions should not lead to controlling them. The link between money and politics should go. Money should not buy influence and different political parties should not be able to spend as they wish on electioneering.

From my uninformed standpoint, it seems to me that dealing with money could be seen as a service, able to charge reasonably for the work done, but with no extra bonuses for bankers and no interest. The gambling side of banking should go.

Indeed, I hope all forms of industrial scale gambling will go. Having a wager may be a matter of innocent fun between friends. It has a long history and will and probably should remain. But National lotteries have been used to raise money usually from the poor for tasks which society as a whole should pay for. And gambling in casinos or on line causes thousands of people deep distress. Gambling also inevitably reinforces the capitalist's damaging obsession with money as the only 'wealth', the route to happiness, with the linked aim of getting rich without working for it.

The third principle addresses how we tackle the two major environmental crises - reducing carbon emissions to net zero and halting the extinction of species with sufficient urgency. Many large infrastructure projects need to be cancelled immediately. When you are in a hole the first step is to stop digging. In future, the carbon costs rather than the economic costs of every policy must be the deciding factor along with yearly caps on the total carbon budgets for different regions. Those agreed at Paris should be increased as the situation is now understood to be more urgent.

Carbon and similar taxes must be used to discourage fossil fuels and every other sort of pollution.

I think space exploration with its inevitably high carbon costs, should be put on hold until we have sorted out the problems of this world. Any suggestion that exploiting space could be a solution should be rejected as absurd and immoral.

The environmental cost in habitat destruction or pollution must also be considered for every policy and action. Two existing principles to protect the environment, the 'precautionary principle', the 'polluter pays principle' must be strictly applied with strong sanctions, and a law against Ecocide introduced.

These principles along with taxes on carbon and pollutants would outlaw nuclear power and GM crops and quickly bring an end to fossil fuel and other damaging industries.

Environmental gain in restorative measures to reduce or capture carbon naturally and reduce pollution in the near future should be supported and rewarded as essential investments.

A major roadblock to these changes will be the big companies profiting from fossil fuels and other polluting industries and those investing in them. They will almost certainly try to delay change or suggest technologies which extend business as usual for them – using coal gas to get hydrogen for example, or promising carbon capture or nuclear fusion to enable current industries to continue.

In this emergency only practical, existing technologies should be used to cut carbon and restore the environment, followed later by research and training into benign alternatives.

Chapter 18   More principles for global reform and roadblocks to it

The fourth principle concerns the interrelationship between the several different global emergencies; global warming, the extinction of species, pandemics, economic collapse, gross inequality, starvation, persecution and war. Governments should accept that these are all linked, so that solutions must be found that tackle them all at the same time. Solutions for one cannot be used if it will make others worse. For example, investing in infrastructure to restore the economy would risk plunging the world into irreversible climate change. Allowing many unnecessary jobs to fail to cut carbon costs risks leaving people to starve. Solutions must be found which address one need in such a way as to solve other problems.

There are several good examples, especially since Covid19 changed the public's behaviour and attitudes. We must use the learning from Covid19 to help in transforming policy.

Transport is one clear example. Transport has been central to global capitalism. The environmental and social costs of transport had never been taken into account. The result has been long supply chains and mass tourism; both of which impact badly on the climate, the environment and societies. Long supply chains are often the result of outsourcing work to where labour costs and working conditions are poor. It's part of the system of exploitation, destroying the living standards of the workers. The UK has outsourced the manufacture of a huge range of products.

Covid19 has revealed the dangers of transport – that it enables the rapid spread of diseases, and that long supply chains are vulnerable to disruption, whether caused by illness or other catastrophes. A chain is only as good as its weakest link. The post Covid19 solution would be for more self-sufficient local communities, dramatically reducing the need for motorised transport. This is exactly what the climate and environment also need, as transport is a major source of many pollutants.

Local production also reduces the risk of crime, such as in the adulteration of food. Covid19 by encouraging local community action has shown how the community can be effective, able to undertake new tasks which will improve their ability to cope in uncertain times.

Policies to combat pandemics will bring social benefits. Covid19 has emphasised the importance of good global health care because we are so interlinked. Viruses do not respect borders. It has also shown how poor living standards and diets make people more vulnerable to disease. Combating pandemics by affordable vaccines and health and social programmes to give decent housing and clean water and air in countries both rich and poor will also improve living standards and lessen inequality, two vital social goals.

Covid19 has shown the importance of many low paid and previously undervalued jobs – cleaning, delivering, care work, etc, as well as the vital contribution of voluntary work. It has exposed the fallacy of the hierarchy of status and rewards in current society. A manager, for example, can get astronomical rewards while workers' pay is not sufficient to live on, despite the fact that the success of the business depends on everyone doing a good job.

In addition, Covid19 and lockdown measures have brought countless job losses, and will almost certainly mean an uncertain job future for individuals (as well as an uncertain workforce available to carry out essential tasks). The climate crises will also make many current jobs untenable. Namely those that cause pollution. There is no evidence that sustainable policies over time will result in fewer jobs. We are facing the monumental task of reform. There will be countless different, essential and worthwhile jobs: for example, in the UK thousands of carers, nurses and teachers as these professions have been grossly understaffed. Everywhere there will be work in renewable and benign industries, dealing with waste, insulating homes, restoring nature, growing healthy food, monitoring the results of policies, etc, etc. And many of these will require funded training.

But in the immediate future thousands will lose their jobs. People in all walks of life must be protected from this economic collapse. The solution is a generous Universal Citizens' Income for everyone as a decent safety net. This takes into account our new understanding of the importance of all levels of work including voluntary work, and the need to slow down the pace of life for the sake of the planet. It should be generous enough for people to live on. It will encourage slow, local living and voluntary work. Critically, it guarantees that no one falls through the net.

It is also the most efficient way of delivery money that will circulate to support the local economy. Means testing to discriminate between different hierarchies of pay is extremely costly. Money goes to administrators, but is lost to the public and their local communities. (The Universal Citizens' Income is described in more detail when considering UK policy, Chapter 19.)

A safe income is just one of the basic needs for individual survival and social harmony. Any responsible government provides food, shelter and water for good health and social stability. Global warming, ecological disaster and current intensive farming practices including GM crops risk widespread starvation. Urgent support must be given to small farmers in the third world who produce most of or food. This will include debt relief and compensation so that these communities can feed themselves before choosing to export. Organic farming, or similar systems to restore soils and biodiversity must be supported everywhere.

The fifth principle addresses the current social crises, the tragedies of inequality, extreme poverty, persecution and war. Many of our institutions and their procedures will continue to act as roadblocks. The slow timetables and processes common in governments and political parties do not have the flexibility or imagination to deal with emergencies.

Global institutions such as the UN and the World Trade organisation are major roadblocks. The World Trade Organisation (WTO) gives overwhelming power to corporations by imposing its rules through its General Agreement on Tariffs and Trade(GATT) (for goods), the General Agreement on Trade in Services (GATS) and Trade-Related Aspects of Intellectual Property Rights (TRIPS). It is central to the exploitative system of capitalism and is destroying societies and the planet. It even allows independent courts to override national sovereignty and fine countries for any losses claimed by corporations to have been caused by national policy.

The UN's principles; together with International Laws to control the conduct of war and the protection of civilians, should provide a fifth principle for the development of a sustainable, civilised way of life. But, it has failed and will continue to fail to do so because it is dominated by a few powerful nations, including the original rogue nuclear states. The veto granted to members of the security council has blocked progress for decades. They have used their powers to pursue competitive ideological wars and what they consider their national interests. Some of its institutions are dominated by wealthy individuals with interests of their own.

At the same time, International Law has been eviscerated because it relies on voluntary compliance and too many nations are still interested in what they see as their 'interests'. Somehow control of the UN and other global institutions must be wrested from malign leaders and International Law must be enforceable. I have no idea how these changes will come, but see global grassroots action as the only way; a demand that these institutions are democratised.

There was and still is a clear desire among the public for effective rules to control the behaviour of nation states, to which we must now add, the behaviour of global corporations.

Critically, effective grassroots demands to change the rules will require widespread education in the North. A recognition of the true history of North/South relations instead of the false myths that have supported colonisation and globalisation for so long. People in rich western countries must recognise that we in the North has not succeeded through our own hard work and intelligence. On the contrary we have prospered, and continue to prosper, from the resources and work of the South.

Historically, the cruel and biased rules of colonisation was the biggest cause of poverty in the South, followed more recently by the equally skewed and barbaric rules of global banking and trade rules. The evidence is that left to themselves the South can do very well. We, in the North, are not kind, nice people offering aid to help those less able, we continue to be ruthless thieves, taking infinitely more than we give.

With Climate Change, the Black Lives Matter movement and similar campaigns, this information is getting through to many in the North. Jason Hickel stresses that people in the South, the majority of the world's population, have been well aware of the gross unfairness of global governance for decades. They have been calling for change for decades, and may take matters into their own hands and impose change. They may refuse to play ball and pay the debt.

If a more educated public in the North join with those of the South, a third attempt to secure civilised global governance could succeed.

Change might start with Ecocide, a law to protect the environment and communities from pollution and habitat destruction. This is now supported by some Western governments, the Pope, thousands of campaigners in the north as well as many governments and small communities in the South. Jason Hickel has suggested three essential policies to transform capitalism by uniting the wishes of millions in both South and North. These would be to cancel debt everywhere, to make minimum wages in each country equal to the medium wage for that country and to democratise global institutions.

The devastation of wars and the brutal treatment of refugees and migrants are two of the most criminal, scandalous and barbaric aspects of our society.

Attitudes to war must change completely. War is the most destructive activity, known to mankind, killing and traumatising people, polluting and destroying the environment, destroying civilisations. The historic use of wars of conquest to acquire territory is no longer reasonable in a world, fully populated, and where we need to co-operate together to save ourselves. War today is suicidal. For any democratic country war should always be the last resort and only to be used in defending its own territory. No other use should be allowed as the purpose of democracy is to decide things by law and negotiation.

Everything about our so called 'defence' policies, and those of our allies, needs to change, not least the distorted language. No longer can attacks on other countries be presented as 'defence'. No longer can 'defending national interests', that is commercial interest or ideologies, be a reason for war. We should accept the basic principle that a defence system should not threaten others instead of the false belief that a big threat brings peace. Nuclear weapons must be outlawed and at the other end of the scale, drone attacks must be recognised as war.

We must recognise that everyone loses in war. Defence spending is a heavy cost and should be the responsibility of each country. It should not be left to corporations, intent on expansion, always developing new weapons to counter new supposed threats.

The current excessive glorification of war and fighters must stop. The only way to honour the sacrifices of the past is to stop sending others to their graves or to suffer trauma. In 'Top Guns and Toxic Waste' Gwyn Prins suggests that army recruits should be used for relief work after catastrophes or to help avoid them. This would be much better for the recruits as well as international relations.

Peacemaking in all its forms must be the way disputes are settled. Techniques for negotiations must be developed and friendly exchanges encouraged. The co-operation required between peoples with very different ideologies to solve our common problems, such as plastic pollution, may help this process. Listening to others, appreciating their perspective, their problems and strengths in order to negotiate a common solution, should aid co-operation.

As part of the same attitude, helping refugees should be seen as a solution to present crises not a problem. Refugees do not choose to leave their homes. They are forced to do so by war, persecution, or extreme poverty and starvation. The richer countries which have produced these conditions should undertake the main task of accepting refugees. They cannot undo past injustices but can accept responsibility for them now. Accepting refugees and treating them well would help to counter very understandable hatred. It would stop recruiting more terrorists. It would help to undo past damage.

It would not be easy. It would be expensive. A great deal of work by professionals and volunteers would be needed to integrate migrants so that they could contribute. And they must be allowed to contribute. Care would be needed to watch out for damaged and dangerous migrants still bent on violence. But it would be moving in the right direction, an ethical policy, a civilising policy, supporting international law and promoting peace.

Providing adequate care would employ many local people. And there would be huge cultural advantages, sharing the rich heritage of other cultures in music, cooking, dancing, poetry and literature and religious festivals.

Enjoying activities together should be a large part of integration. Enjoying the differences, will show us the similarities. This is perfectly possible. There are many examples of tolerant communities where different ethnic and religious groups have lived together in harmony and enjoyed each other's festivals.

At the same time richer countries with aging populations would gain willing and able workers. Adult migrants are an asset. Both because the costs of their childhood and training have been covered by their native country and because they have usually been among the most able and ambitious. With their talents they have contributed greatly to the life of their adopted countries. We should welcome them, particularly when the huge reforms needed to our way of life are likely to need a huge workforce.

Freedom of movement must be protected for everyone as a basic right. How ludicrous that, now travel is easy, it becomes controlled and forbidden! Globalisation has led to families being spread across the world, with countless mixed race families. Making it difficult for them to see each other would be a new form of cruelty. Travel is polluting, but over time perhaps airships could be developed to cut carbon emissions dramatically. My father who built aerodromes and flew tiger moths, said that safe airships were on the brink of being developed when war broke out with its need for speed.

Freedom of movement is particularly important for those facing persecution. In today's interconnected world, ideas get everywhere. As a result, priorities and morals are changing rapidly, too rapidly for some countries trying to maintain their identity. Cruel, sometimes deadly, persecution is common. Enabling the persecuted to live elsewhere is not only kind to them and likely to bring benefits to the countries they adopt, but will also reduce tensions in the countries they have left, and may eventually encourage more tolerance.

Chapter 19 The Opposing Roles of Science – The Cause of Global Crises; The Solution to Global Crises, and Roadblocks to it

Science is a two edged sword. The good or harm caused depends on where it is directed. The huge expansion of medical knowledge seems an obvious good, but the equally huge expansion in warfare, ways of killing, has added to the trauma, death and destruction of countless people.

Over the past decades science has revolutionised our lives, now controlling almost everything we do or get in richer countries - from the water we drink, the transport we use, our heating, our light, the houses we live in, our health system, our entertainment, our communication and control systems, etc. It has achieved amazing feats of accuracy such as space travel and has understandable authority.

It has made many aspects of life easier and more pleasant. But at the same time, in direct contrast, the scale of interference in natural systems enabled by science and technology and driven by capitalist greed is the major cause of global warming, the extinction of species, pandemics and the associated social distress.

Scientific knowledge changes. What is accepted at one time is proved wrong later. Science is an exploration, an uncertain journey continually finding out new facts and developing new explanations. Scientists follow a set method. First they collect and measure information. Then make a 'hypothesis' – a guess to explain the facts identified. And then test this hypothesis by making predictions about related facts which would fit with it.

The strongest support for a theory comes if its predictions are fulfilled – such as in the case of Global Warming. When predictions fail, the scientists start again with a new hypothesis and more information.

Collaboration with others to check the accuracy of measurements and explore other hypotheses is essential.

Early support for fossil fuels and chemical pesticides could be understood as an inadequate understanding of the consequences, both for global warming and for the destruction of soils. It was part of the journey in scientific knowledge which continues to revolutionise our understanding of many natural processes.

It is certainly true that the unintended consequences of new inventions or processes frequently cause problems – they become time bombs - as they not noticed for far too long. But this cannot explain why two damaging industries were allowed to exist for so long. The answer has to be corruption - the abuse of science to support financial interests. Spurious scientific arguments used by large corporations or governments have proved devastating. Deliberate lies, denying known dangers is all too common.

Scientists have proved to be no better than others. Just as willing to lie for personal advantage. The tobacco and fossil fuel industries provide two terrible examples. Their scientists were well aware of the dangers, but used their authority for decades to conceal the dangers of tobacco and global warming. They deliberately confused the public in well resourced campaigns. The Thalidomide scandal of the 50 and 60s is an earlier example.

Telling lies, or concealing the truth about dangers, is widespread in many industries including the nuclear industries and GM. I was at a meeting at the John Innes Research Centre in Norwich, ostensibly called to inform farmers about GM but which clearly failed to do so. They claimed GM was just like normal plant breeding, but more accurate and much quicker. Having just been to a talk by Dr John Latham, a plant virologist, as part of a local consultation on GMOs, I knew this to be completely untrue.

At a later talk, given to the 'Friends of John Innes', the emphasis was quite different - all about their influence on government, boasting of their meetings with Tony Blair. This stark contrast to their earlier claim to be 'simple' scientists fits with the covert and corrupt influence big companies have on governments described in the Corbett report.

Lying scientists pose a very real problem. How are lay people to judge what is happening? One answer is to ask who is making claims and what if anything they stand to gain from it. Could they have they been bought? But it is also true that those in an industry are best placed to know the facts. There is no simple answer.

In this uncertainty it is quite easy for people to deride scientific knowledge and warnings in one area, even though they, like the rest of us, rely on science in so many other areas of life. Listening to lots of views, particularly independent views and whistle blowers, would seem sensible. The current emergencies have produced hundreds of scientists willing to share their information for the common good, such as those listed in 'Drawdown'.

Another deliberate tactic used by big corporations is to buy up patents of sustainable alternatives to stop their production.

The scale and speed of diversification and specialisation over the last few decades has increased the risk of unintended consequences. Both the public and government are unaware of what many processes and products are and their consequences. Our treatment of waste over the last decades is a sad example. While the unintended consequences of the computer controls and artificial intelligence so prevalent today is still largely unknown – a time bomb to come.

There are obvious benefits in the speed of calculations, but also obvious dangers from the use of algorithms which lack sensitivity. The authority given to artificial intelligence is very worrying and unwarranted. After all, a computer can only carry out instructions that have been put in by people, possibly the thoughts of just one person or a small group. Yet once in a computer their output seems to gain widespread legal authority. It may be used to control policies. Artificial intelligence, almost certainly misnamed, is undemocratic. Secrecy about the instructions given and a general ignorance about what this means, seems a major danger. Relying on computers as we do also makes us vulnerable to interference of any sort, from malfunctions and electrical breakdown to criminal activity.

Another roadblock; scientists even with the best of intentions are influenced or intimidated by the zeitgeist – the norms, aspirations and limitations of current thinking. For example, some animal researchers failed to describe 'human like' behaviours as they were afraid they wouldn't be believed.

The arrogance of 'accepted' science is a major roadblock. It is common for scientists to refuse to accept findings unless they can 'explain' them in terms of their own scientific models. In this way they have failed to recognise many excellent solutions. In global terms, it is a tragedy for us all that the expertise of peasant farmers and health practices based on generations of experience, have been denied and the more destructive practices of western 'science' supported. All the more surprising since many of our drugs have been developed from plants used by indigenous people. (This particular arrogance was of course promoted strongly by the scientific teaching initiated by those profiting from it, as described in Chp 11.)

Vandana Shiva points out that western science, as applied to farming, has been dominated by Darwin's ideas of competition and Newtonian-Cartesian theories of separate atoms. These views have been overtaken by new scientific knowledge. Quantum physics teaches us that the world is made 'of fields of potential with a dynamic transformation of particles into waves' and vice versa. Not separate atoms. Quantum physics is all about inseparability. Ecology similarly teaches that 'everything is a web of life.' 'Gaia is a self-organising system at every level from the cell to the organism to the planet'. Co-operation and interdependence are as important as competition, if not more so. Epigenetics teaches us that 'the environment influences genes', which 'do not regulate or organize themselves independent of the environment'. (Who Really Feeds the World).

In other words, she explains how the 'science' of industrial farming was false, and modern western science is now catching up with the fact that traditional peasant farming embodied our best scientific knowledge, although it was not labelled as such. (The same processes may follow regarding medical practice, which have been equally influenced by the oligarchs' funded teaching.)

On a much smaller scale, many of us will have suffered the same fate as a friend of mine. Years ago, when suffering from excruciating pain was told she was imagining it because the medical knowledge of that time failed to identify the cause. Later improvements allowed the cause to be identified.

The belief that progress in science will solve present problems is equally dangerous. It has legitimised nuclear power when we have no safe way of containing the waste. It is the false assurance that will be used by those who do not want to undertake the scale of social reform needed in the present crises.

The way scientific discoveries are reported has become another road block to reform as it has led to a general mistrust of scientists. The media and governments do not seem to understand the uncertainty of scientific progress. They both confidently issue headline warnings and advice, which are then frequently contradicted. This inaccuracy has made the public distrust science, which climate change deniers and fossil fuel investors have used to their advantage.

Finally, a different type of roadblock. The speed of scientific development and techniques has produced cultural difficulties that cause tensions which hamper co-operation. Rapid changes in society in the UK and similar countries, for example, have come from easy and accessible contraception, abortions, as well as fertility treatment, sex changes and implanted eggs. Some people adapt quickly, others don't. Not everyone in these societies has celebrated these changes, with homophobia and anti-abortions protests common.

The situation is far worse in other countries because of the clash of cultures that has followed globalisation. Individuals in many countries with very different faiths and social traditions have been influenced by ideas from the democratic west. Tensions arise in communities and families where some are in favour of western ideas and others hostile to them. The hostility is not surprising. The cultural identity and social norms of many countries and faiths are threatened by these new ideas. It is not surprising, for example, that societies that value privacy find many western blatant sexual habits shocking. When these seem to be imposed by the dominating capitalist West, hostility and more extreme religious views and cultural rules are an understandable reaction.

In general our huge scientific understanding of ourselves and of nature, together with the lessons of history, can either be used destructively to control and exploit, or can be used constructively and with some humility to build tolerant, peaceful societies, cooperating and respecting other cultures and nature.

One big problem shown by learning experiments is our difficulty in thinking ahead about new problems. We learn quickly to change behaviour if we are hurt, to avoid fire for example. We respond well to immediate situations and ones that we can predict from our past, but are very slow at anticipating new problems. This is a real dilemma now as reacting to catastrophic climate change and species extinction will come too late. We desperately need to think ahead.

We know that human behaviour can be cruel, vicious and supremely selfish, but also gentle, generous, kind and altruistic, able to perform huge feats of endurance for the benefit of others. Nothing should surprise us about the huge range of human potential. Science has added to this knowledge. It has taught us that we are part of the animal kingdom, sharing most of our DNA with many species not just with closely related primates. We think of ourselves as cultured, removed from animal behaviour. But knowing how animal we are can explain many of our reactions. They seem hard wired, based on our animal nature and include a huge variety of behaviours. Many could be described as selfish, aimed at an individual's survival, but many other seem altruistic. I am sure many of us recognised a kinship with animal behaviours shown in David Attenborough's wildlife programmes.

The most devastating 'animal' response to human society is how quickly we turn to fighting and killing over disagreements, conflicts of interest or greed. This primitive behaviour is directly opposed to the ideals of democracy and the greatest danger to civilisation. Religion and race are often blamed as the causes of violence, but peaceful stable communities of very mixed groups have existed and are perfectly possible. I think it may be more a case that once violence starts it degenerates into primitive tribal behaviour of one sort or another. But I suspect an underlying and unacknowledged grievance may often have initiated the trouble.

This seemed reflected from an account from the USSR in the 80s, when it was breaking up. A professor of History from Tashkent was in London for a year's study and could not believe the press reports of racial tension. When she left there had been no sign of it. A very mixed community of Usbeks, Armenians, Russians, Jews and others lived together apparently easily, uninterested in nationality or religion. Many families were a mixture. Yet when she returned, as if out of the blue, gangs of Usbeks stole cars and attacked homes with the compliance of the police. The tension was echoed in Moscow where Russians were unwilling to offer homes to any who were not pure Russian.

I heard a similar story from Yugoslavia. A highly qualified vet who had travelled in all the different parts of Yugoslavia with no difficulties happened to be in the UK when war broke out. He admitted to being totally surprised, aware only of some small disturbance in the army. Governments must learn from such examples to ensure fair social conditions which do not allow grievances and violence to flourish.

Lastly, science and history have also taught us about unhelpful thinking processes - our tendency to 'blame'; the way we assume 'intentions'; how we interpret actions to fit our prejudices; the classic mistake of thinking our enemy's enemy is our friend; the power of manipulative slogans and repetition to control ideas, 'the word is god', etc. It is the task of governments now to use hindsight and scientific knowledge to encourage behaviours which will enable our survival - tolerance, co-operation, flexibility, openness and intelligence.

Chapter 20 The UK is a Special Case. Urgent Reforms – Voting, Basic Income and Housing.

Change has to be global. Nothing less has any chance of even limited success at this late stage.   Change has to come at every level of organisation - individual, community, national, international and global levels. Reforms in the UK, as everywhere, need to obey the essential global principles already outlined.

But in the UK we have a particularly hard task. We are a special case. We have to face not just the global crises but also the domestic crises of ruined services, gross inequality and poverty caused by Austerity, and the economic uncertainty of Brexit.   All this with the disadvantage of an unrepresentative, incompetent and ideology driven government which will be hard to get rid of. We need drastic reform, but it is hard to see a way forward.

This and the two following chapters list the kind of essential reforms which an ethical government could be expected to introduce to solve the global and domestic problems. It has been compiled from the ideas of many grass roots campaigns as well as those of more formal bodies. It is not suggested as a final or even the best list. My knowledge is patchy, and the world is changing so fast and knowledge is increasing so fast that very different solutions may be more effective.

Clearly any rational or ethical government would introduce a proportional voting system. The present government is very unlikely to do so willingly. An obvious solution would be for all other parties to join together in an alliance for one election to gain the majority. This was proposed as the Progressive Alliance for the 2017 election, but the Labour party refused to join in. Without a coalition we are stuck. If the government has its way, the next election will be nearly 4 years off.

In any event a proportional voting system is not a quick fix. The changes in the thinking and behaviour of MPs to allow consensual politics are likely to take some time. But it would put us on the path to be a more civilised and a more educated country.

A variety of new ideas could be aired and false myths challenged. It would encourage the break up of the big parties and the culture of lying that has gone with that. MPs should be able to join smaller parties that share their views.

Telling the truth would be liberating, both for politicians and for the listening public. When one party does not gain an overall majority, very common with proportional representation, a consensus will need to be negotiated. Co-operation rather than insults should eventually become habitual.

Much more urgent is the introduction of a Citizens' Income, as both a moral and a practical step. The Citizens' Income gives a guaranteed income to everyone, children included, with extra support for the ill and disabled. It would be a transformative policy, a major factor in enabling change.

It corrects the basic fallacy of capitalism that only paid work is of value. In the context of climate and ecological breakdown and the economic devastation of Covid19, it will be invaluable in several ways. It will support people facing economic ruin. No one knows how many jobs will go. No one knows how many businesses will collapse or for how long this will go on. But our knowledge of the limited capacity of the world tells us that many jobs should go and many businesses should collapse. They are unsustainable, causing climate breakdown.

A realistic universal basic income will protect people during these changes and it will ensure that employers have to pay realistic wages for necessary tasks. It will end the subsidy to businesses given through tax credits.

In the UK it will be essential to tackle the extreme inequality, poverty and distress caused by the years of punitive austerity cuts in benefits and the inadequate and uncertain wages for 'the working poor'. By ending poverty and giving dignity to the vulnerable it will reduce stress and improve mental health.

It will counter the inequality which has caused so much anger and distress in our society. Covid19 has shown the fallacy of unequal status, whereby one man at the top is paid huge sums for the success of the whole organisation, (even when it fails). While the work of the many who contributed to the success is ignored and they are underpaid. Covid19 has shown us that those doing mundane and low paid jobs are just as valuable, as are those working voluntarily. The Citizens' Income reflects this fact.

By investing in people it will counter the long term government policy to reduce the number of people employed, by having fewer larger institutions and demanding more of each worker. Governments have seen people as a 'cost', while infrastructure is an 'investment'. A policy leading to more travel and stressed workers.

The Citizen's Income has become more important as so many jobs are lost to artificial intelligence. And in the present set of crises, it will also enable many more to take part in thinking about political solutions through local groups or citizens assemblies, as part of a participatory democracy. Something clearly needed as the top down control of party politics in government has failed us so badly.

By enabling people to survive without all consuming paid work, it will encourage voluntary work and should allow a flowering of talent and creativity.

To be effective it must be enough to live on. It will enable people to live slowly and more locally, which is essential to reverse climate breakdown, and a good protection against pandemics. Strong communities would have a chance to develop to help in any future uncertainties.

Although the Citizens' Income will be expensive, there will be savings. As a universal benefit, it will be easier and therefore cheaper to administer, unlike complicated sectional means tested support. Many costs will be recouped by progressive taxation of the better off. It is also relevant that the extra money paid to those choosing to stay at home will almost certainly circulate through the local economy, supporting many others.

Some resent the idea that a universal benefit will allow people to be apparently lazy; doing nothing. That is a capitalist fallacy. Caring for families is real work. We should be grateful to anyone who is content to live in a modest way, as their slow living will help to avert climate catastrophe.

It is relevant that the Citizens' Income was proposed decades ago as a solution to the 'Poverty Trap'. It was recognised that people on benefits could not afford to take jobs because their benefits were cut just when they had new expenses - clothing, fares, equipment, etc. The Citizens' Income was seen as a way to help people get back to work.

All the pilot projects on various forms of Citizens' Income around the world have confirmed that people like to do worthwhile jobs. They like to be involved with others. The Citizens' income will not encourage dependence on the state as some argue, but will allow people to choose the best, most productive, life for themselves – to take paid work or to study, or develop businesses or their talents.

A moral case for a Citizens' Income comes from the fact that we are restricted in what we can do in a modern society. We have to fit in with its many rules and regulations. The Citizens' Income can be seen as a contract by which we give up a large part of our independence in return for an allowance to allow a modest but decent life.

Also it is morally correct to share today's wealth, which comes largely from the accumulated knowledge and technical advances made by countless people in previous generations.

We know that more recent developments have often been supported by tax payers' money. For example, the Guardian (16 April 2021) reported that the Oxford/AstraZeneca vaccines for Covid19 have been funded overwhelmingly by tax payers and charitable trusts, with industry only supplying 2.8% of the cost. Clearly wealth should not be captured by the few as if it is all their own work.

It is interesting to look at ideas of human happiness and how these relate to current policies and the alternative of a universal Citizen's Income.

I first learned of the psychologist Maslow's 'Hierarchy of Needs' in the 60s. It is still relevant today. He identified a 'Hierarchy of Needs' for human happiness, in which the most basic needs had to be met before people could move on to achieving higher ones.

Maslow stressed that every person is capable of, and has the desire, to move up the hierarchy toward a level of 'self-actualization'. Unfortunately, progress is often disrupted by a failure to meet lower level needs. Life experiences, such as divorce, loss of a job, accidents, and, we may add, government policies, may stop their progress.

Most basic is the physiological need for food, warmth, shelter, rest, to which we might add clean air and water. After this comes the need for safety and security and some predictability in our lives. The third level is the need for love and feelings of belonging, intimate relationships, family and friends, community. Once these are relatively satisfied comes the need for esteem, prestige and feeling of accomplishment. It is followed by the highest level in the hierarchy that of self-actualisation, feelings of autonomy. In other words, being able to make choices to achieve ones full potential including the whole range of creative activities.

In the UK today, the cruelty of austerity and many other policies has stopped people being able to live as they would wish. Many are denied even basic physical needs and security. In contrast the Citizens' Income provides basic needs and security, the two lowest levels. It allows people time to enjoy emotional ties with family, friends and neighbours. And finally it offers autonomy, choices to enable people to fulfil their potential.

On its own the Citizens' Income will not do enough. It will need to be accompanied by other policies. In particular by a reformed housing policy or much of the income will go on rents to private landlords.

Urgent reform of housing is vital both for people and for the planet. The social value of good housing cannot be overestimated. It should be the right of every citizen in a rich country like our own. The insecure, unhealthy, overcrowded and dangerous housing and homelessness many suffer today is a scandal. It is the root cause of many other social problems – violence, drug dependency, ill health, crime and even death. Lockdown during Covid19 has made the need for improvement even more obvious. Any ethical government must tackle this shameful situation as a priority.

It will be a huge and tricky task because of competing needs. Millions of new homes of a decent standard are needed for the homeless and the hidden homeless – those forced to share cramped, unhealthy and dangerous houses and flats. The need to cut carbon, means standards must now include energy efficiency and insulation in all houses and the use of low carbon materials, such as wood, in new build.

An obvious solution would have been a to build a huge number of eco-council houses with reasonable rents, both to provide enough homes and to destroy the monopoly of private landlords.

However, in the present climate crises this is not possible. We have to apply strict yearly constraints on carbon emissions to meet the Paris Climate Accord limits, which means minimum building. Equally important, we need to keep land to grow food and restore our countryside which prohibits building on green field sites.

It is clear that existing buildings should be adapted wherever possible to satisfy the desperate need for housing. This could include empty buildings, second homes, shops and hotels. The economic turndown after Covid19 could provide all sorts of buildings for housing, all those no longer economically viable as shops or businesses.

Aiming for a society of home owners must go. Home ownership will continue, but the government's role should be in rented homes. Housing should again become a service, controlled by the needs of people and society. It should be a local service. Only the people on the ground know what is needed and what resources they have.

Councils will have to regain the expertise they have lost. Luckily, Covid19 has proved how fast extraordinary things can be achieved and how willing people are to share knowledge. Councils must work with local people and try different methods to get the best results. There is a wealth of knowledge about carbon efficient building and planning techniques to be learnt and shared.

Self-build is one possibility, cheap and empowering for the builders. Young foreign workers may prove their worth.

Chapter 21   Further essential reforms in the UK - energy and transport

Policies on energy, and transport need to be reformed as a matter of urgency to combat climate change and species extinction and because they have also failed the public.

Many changes suggested now, along with housing reform, were advocated by Lord Sterne back in 2008 to restore the economy after the banking collapse and prevent climate breakdown. It is tragic that his advice was ignored and we have suffered instead the devastation of austerity and privatisation. But the advice applies in most cases just as much to the present economic recession caused by Covid19 and is even more urgent now. A policy shift to a green economy would produce countless jobs, mostly local jobs, right across the UK in insulating homes, making cycles, mopeds and wind turbines, and trains and buses, although public transport may prove more difficult with social distancing. Old fashioned railway carriages to isolate small groups may come back.

In energy policy, applying the 'precautionary principle' would eliminate both nuclear power and fossil fuels. Nuclear power because it is just too dangerous and fossil fuels because they cause global warming.   All subsidies should stop immediately. A carbon tax should discourage any production which should be phased out as soon as possible

All emphasis should be on energy saving, the development of benign renewables and the use of electricity to provide heating and transport. Electric buses, vans and cars should be developed until and unless a better alternative is available. Replacing petrol engines with electric ones in existing cars should be used as the most efficient method, instead of manufacturing a whole lot of new cars with all the embedded carbon that entails.

Two existing models suggesting pathways forward are recorded by Professor Catherine Rowett in 'Energising the East'. The National Grid uses decentralised onshore community wind as the quickest way to cut carbon to reach net zero by 2050. Onshore wind is the cheapest, most efficient source, best for the local economy and increasing public awareness.

Their plan demands a simpler planning process, with grants and subsidies to encourage a speedy transformation. It also requires a growth in battery storage, to replace gas by addressing intermittency of generation; and a local distribution network to integrate storage in EVs (electric cars), which can supply energy back into the network. EVs left plugged in when not in use can both charge from the network, and discharge when additional power is needed.

The second model aims to produce zero carbon by 2030. The Centre for Alternative Technology (CAAT), uses a combination of energy saving, the development of benign renewables, and the use of electricity to provide heating such as air source heat pumps, and transport.

Solar should be restricted to roofs rather than taking up land needed for crops and the natural environment. Grants for roof solar panels should make this available for all.

The Severn Barrage should be approved and research and development into other tidal and wave systems increased.

The emphasis on the cheapest possible electricity, would rule out private providers. Electricity should be nationalised. There is no place for private profits in a service industry. Local government would need to be involved in a decentralised system.

Energy saving affects many sectors. It means more efficient equipment, the re-use and repair of equipment, an end to built in obsolescence, an end to continuous upgrades with earlier models not supported, and massive insulation in properties. Overall it means producing less. Cutting consumption, on the assumption that the world can sustain our needs but not our greed.

Before the Covid19 crisis, the main suggestion for cutting carbon costs in transport was to encourage a move to more efficient public transport. This may have to be reconsidered given the risks of infection in trains and buses. The main focus with transport now should be to use Planning Policy to cut the need for all types of motor vehicles, including electric cars, because all have carbon costs and are polluting.

The planning system needs to make essential services accessible locally, in contrast to the existing pattern of shutting local services in favour of larger, more distant establishments, whether hospitals, schools, courts, or shops, etc.

A more local society of smaller units will be vital to combat climate change, pollution and the danger of pandemics. It will help to build stronger local communities able to take responsibility for themselves and offer solutions. If recycling for example, was the responsibility of local areas, there would be a big incentive to develop imaginative ways to re-use products and to persuade businesses to cut and standardise packaging to reduce the cost to themselves. Sharing ideas which is now so easy with the internet would hasten helpful changes.

Many things learnt during the Covid19 lockdown encourage helpful change. We have learnt how much work can be done at home to cut down on commuting; how many meetings can be held virtually instead of in person; how schooling can be aided by virtual lessons.

By emptying the roads lockdown allowed cycling to increase. The improved air quality has highlighted the personal cost of pollution. Increasing dramatically the number of cycle and pedestrian ways would significantly cut carbon emissions and transform our towns, while improving people's health.

Covid19 has highlighted the role of air traffic in spreading viruses, which should make people think twice before going on long range flights, particularly for short holiday breaks, and business conferences. All these improvements need to be incorporated into new ways of safer living. A fair tax on fuel would lead to a dramatic and healthy drop in air traffic.

Covid19 and the subsequent lockdown has also made us more aware of the many risks of sea transport; in spreading viruses, in carbon emissions, in damaging life in the oceans and in the risk of disruptions and delays to deliveries. Several more reasons to be more self-sufficient, to grow more of our food and make more of the things we need. Increasing difficulties for trading that may follow Brexit will make self-sufficiency all the more important.

An ethical government would do everything it could to support local living, creating healthy homes and a pleasant local environment.

Chapter 22 Further Essential reforms in the UK – Health and Food Production

Reclaiming the Health Service from the ravages of privatisation and central control started by Margaret Thatcher and continued by succeeding governments, should be a clear priority. Its weaknesses have been fully exposed by Covid 19, although they were evident well before.

It is important to remember that the UK had a Health Service to be proud of. The NHS, set up after the second world war as a central part of the welfare state, was popular with the public and credited with giving good value. It was a national service free to those who needed it, paid for out of taxes and administered through local areas. It was still a two tier system with private patients able to access treatments quicker and some specialised treatments.

The last 70 years have seen an extraordinary expansion in medical knowledge and treatments, which would clearly need considerably increased funding, especially given our ageing population. But since the 1980s political decisions and cuts in funding have brought the NHS to its knees. Once again the reforms needed will be rolling back on the ideological changes imposed by governments.

Restoring our failing system will take time, money and effort. A priority should be funding adequate pay for all who work in the NHS, adequate facilities and training. Also funding local authorities to provide adequate social care.

Another priority should be ending privatisation, with no new contracts given and no existing contracts renewed.

As soon as possible, the organisation of the NHS should be returned to local authorities funded by central government.

The global power of big pharma should be challenged in collaboration with other governments and the UN. The development of drugs by universities and similar organisations, should be supported. Reasonable payments for drugs should cover all the costs of production, but not include profits. Lobbying by pharmaceuticals should be limited and MPs with interest in private medicine should not be allowed to vote on anything that affects the NHS.

As soon as possible, free access to dentistry should be restored and mental health and drug rehabilitation given the same level of provision as physical health, which will entail a huge expansion of services.

These reforms would provide millions of caring jobs, in contrast to the severe cuts suffered over the last years. Cutting manpower has been the major way to cut costs, in the name of efficiency. Instead, it has lowered the standards of services and induced stress in workers. Happily, caring jobs of all kinds are not usually associated with high carbon emissions. They will become part of a sustainable society.

Providing for a healthy lifestyle with access to sport and recreation and healthy living conditions should become part of health policy. As should a healthy diet, something many doctors have been very ignorant about. In contrast the Ayurveda medical tradition sees the daily diet and the cook as the first line of defence for good health.

Recognising that a global world, with global diseases needs a global system of health care for the good of everyone, the government should work with others and the UN to produce effective medicines and facilities for all countries, including poorer ones. Cancelling all the debt should be an essential part of this policy along with the aid programs local people want.

Over time alternative and complimentary therapies should be included in the NHS. Herbal medicine for example has helped people for thousands of years. In other countries complimentary medicines are respected by their modern health systems. For example, as long ago as the 1950's my late father-in-law was advised by his Swiss doctors to try acupuncture, as their drugs could not save his leg. It worked and for decades after that he had follow up treatments whenever bad circulation threatened to lead to gangrene.

In this country I have every reason to be grateful to the NHS. It has saved my life on more than one occasion and continues to support me with drugs and equipment. But I have also relied on help from acupuncture, osteopathy and herbal medicine for issues the NHS could not address and to help counter the effects of NHS drugs. The hostility of many doctors to alternative therapies is misplaced, especially when NHS treatments so often have harmful side effects.

The health of the nation relies on nutrition. The UK is known for the high consumption of unhealthy fast food. But one good result of the Covid19 lockdown has been the way many people have enjoyed simple home cooking, fresh fruit and veg and even growing food.

We need to produce good food urgently both for people and the environment. An ethical government should stop all research and production of GM crops and use taxation and regulation to discourage all forms of intensive farming with animals or crops. This would avoid dangerous chemicals in crops and hormones and anti-biotics in animals, as well as improve animals' lives.

The government should support a return to organic farming and research into natural systems of breeding, crop rotation and intercropping, to increase yields and control pests as well as to restore the soil. As market gardening is one of the most productive systems, it should expand allotments so that people can grow their own food. This would also increase the resilience of local communities. Maybe community allotments could be used to encourage more people to grow their own.

Meat production should to be cut significantly because it is less efficient. Rearing meat uses more vegetables than would be needed if we just ate the vegetables. But this does not mean people have to go vegetarian or vegan. Animals fed on natural foods are part of a benign natural cycle which increases biodiversity.

The distance foods are transported is highly relevant. Transport is carbon heavy. The aim should be to have food consumed as near as possible to where it is grown. Where foreign foods are essential or part of long history, the most efficient form of transport should be used.

The healthiest food for people and the planet is organic, fresh, seasonal and unprocessed. Local food production should be the aim, which also makes criminal activity easier to control, while providing local jobs. Local shops, farm shops and markets should be supported to provide food in contrast to supermarkets which have a heavy carbon footprint and where profits usually go out of the local area.

It is ironic that nowadays supermarkets are usually promoted as providing jobs. Yet at first they were promoted for being cheaper because customers picked their own shopping, saving the cost of shop assistants. Having destroyed many local businesses, supermarkets are now almost certainly not any cheaper than many other shops.

A functioning system of inspection should be re-installed to stop criminals degrading food. Processing should be recognised as carbon intensive and taxed as such.

Chapter 23 Essential reform of UK Education and Justice Systems

A reformed education system will be vital for the changes we need. We must roll back the central control and market ideology that have given us overcrowded classes, school exclusions and distressed students and teachers, despite all the expertise and work of teachers.

Education must provide pupils with the knowledge and ability to understand and contribute to the sort of society needed now. This is not as urgent as the need to provide adequate housing and incomes, or to cut carbon with new energy and transport policies or to restore the NHS and provide good food, but it is no less important in the long run.

An ethical government should provide a rounded education, with reasonable class sizes, full of sport and the arts, driven by the considerable knowledge of teachers with the involvement of parents and local people. It should return to being a local service. To do this, many features of the existing system, indeed, the whole purpose of the changes of recent governments, will need to be undone.

The first steps should restore grants for further education for students and security and decent pay for teachers and lecturers, (but not the excessive pay given to Vice Chancellors and the like); an end to routine SATs tests and the excessive paper work for teachers, who would be trusted to do their job rather than having to do it and then prove they have.

The National Curriculum should go. There never was any need for one. It was a means of promoting a particular ideology and increasing central control. National exams during and at the end of the school journey were a sufficient national standard and would become so again, unless or until other means of assessment are developed.

Over time private schools of all types should go. This includes 'Public' schools, which offer class advantage to the rich. Once they are part of general education, the rich, with their lobbying capacity, will be keen to have good standards everywhere. This seemed true in Germany. I was an au pair to a titled German family in the 60s. Their children went automatically to the local village school.

Other schools to be closed should include Faith schools which reinforce racial and religious differences, Free Schools and Acadamies, part of the government's policy to fragment and privatise education while bringing it under central government control. There should be no place for profit in education, nor for class division, nor for the rivalry between schools caused by the 'market' which has led to many children being excluded.

In the long run children from different faiths and different incomes should be taught together. That is the best, maybe the only way to overcome prejudice and hostility. The required changes in cooking arrangements and day time routines would be expensive, but would teach all children about other ways of life and bring different groups of adults together, too.

Education should return to local authorities working transparently with teachers and parents. Flexibility in a decentralised system would encourage sharing ideas to promote the best solutions.

Many syllabuses would need to change to reflect the world we live in accurately. History for example to include the real facts of colonialism and slavery, and, in this global world, it should also include more Information from other countries.

The climate and ecological disasters have revealed a deep ignorance of the natural world we depend on. Natural history would be an important subject giving children direct experience of animals and plants.

The total ignorance most of the public display about how our systems of government work should prompt teaching about it at Secondary Schools. The teaching of economics for older children and adults should change completely. It needs to reflect systems which work for people and the globe.

All this is a very tall order and it is equally important not to overwhelm children with facts. There is so much to learn that school can only be a beginning. It needs to give children the basic techniques and knowledge to investigate. Learning should be seen as a life long activity and an enjoyable one.

The size of schools is relevant. Covid19 has shown the risk of large numbers of people mixing. Climate change and Covid19 both require less transport. Smaller more local schools should be built, and more teachers trained to allow smaller class sizes.

The asset of expert online teaching developed during lockdown should become a permanent part of the system.

Similarly, the market ideology should no longer dominate universities. Blue sky research should be funded again instead of the emphasis on business links and short term profits. Wide spread co-operation between universities should be supported, rather than the competition of today. Famous scientists have pointed out how many important discoveries in the past relied on blue sky funding and are impossible under today's rules.

Restoring a fair system of law and order should be central to reforms. An independent strong judiciary is at the basis of democracy. What is 'right' in any situation must be decided by agreed laws, and made available to all. Justice must be seen to be delivered in every way – whether by laws, by lawyers and judges through the courts and judicial review; or by the police, prisons, probation service, or by forensic science, or by international law.

Reforms are urgently needed to address the current shameful situation in domestic law which is, unfair, brutal, brutalising and increases the danger to the public. Once again, the reforms will need to undo the changes brought about by austerity cuts and privatisation in every part of the justice system. We must recognise that justice is expensive and cannot be done on the cheap. Adequate funding is needed for legal aid, for lawyers, police, and prison officers, as well as improved facilities.

But this will not be enough. Our attitude to crime and its prevention should change completely. We must recognise that crime is often caused and is certainly encouraged by social factors. Criminals are often victims of social failure. All the factors causing stress in society; inequality, poverty, homelessness and overcrowded housing and the lack of facilities for sport or recreation, tend to lead to higher crime and violence, including domestic violence.

So crime prevention, just like good health, should become part of all policies, from housing, to benefits, to schooling and recreation; which all need adequate funds and facilities.

Drugs and mental illness are particular issues. Drug dependency drives many crimes and drugs in prisons increase the danger there. Similarly, many in prison are suffering from mental illness. All these people should be treated for their health issues to prevent many crimes.

In another major reform 'reparation' should become the aim of the criminal justice system (as highlighted by the Green Party). Using the principle of 'restorative justice' it denounces crimes but deals constructively with both the victim and the offender. It aims to heal the rifts caused by crimes; to help social integration and to integrate offenders rather than outlaw them.

In such a system, the community's first response to a crime is to offer support and services to victims. All who admit their offence or are convicted would immediately be provided with an opportunity to offer reparation to their victim(s). Local mediation services working with victim support, would negotiate between the two parties, offering the chance of a direct meeting if the victim wanted one. The community would have the responsibility of providing adequate support.

Community Service and Probation would continue to be used, but fines would be replaced by reparation wherever possible. The emphasis would be on increasing reconciliation and reducing detention.

Intervention would be as little as the seriousness of the offence would allow. When prison is needed for the protection of others, the prisoner would not be degraded or humiliated. Their human rights would be recognised and every effort made to rehabilitate them, including education.

The police are the face of the law seen by most people. The police need to be trusted. Policing should be by the consent of the community. There should be more local police stations and part-time and community police officers from a wide range of backgrounds and experience.

They should be accountable to local government. Any accusation of police criminality, corruption and racism should be dealt with by an independent authority. Police should be charged and investigated in the same manner as any other person.

Police should get training and support to help them deal with racial and religious intolerance, homophobia and with vulnerable people, including children, both in the police force and in the community at large. They should be involved in crime prevention.

Decades of crimes against children and other vulnerable people have been particularly shameful. The prevalence of child abuse should be acknowledged and addressed by society as a whole. With more education to increase awareness, as well as taking complaints seriously and screening those who have significant contact with children or any vulnerable person. Similarly bullying attitudes to women need to be addressed by the police and by society in general.

Critically the whole range of international law should be supported. There is no other way to restore civilised behaviour among different countries.

The UK government should work with other countries to strengthen the law, but there are several immediate steps to take. The government should honour the Non-Proliferation Treaty and get rid of our nuclear weapons. It should cancel any recent legislation or proposals which have undermined international humanitarian law such as giving our soldiers immunity from prosecution. It should obey its commitments under international and domestic law to offer proper asylum to refugees.

International justice would also be involved in instigating a truly ethical 'defence' policy to cut arms manufacture and stop war crimes and other illegal attacks on other countries and peoples.

These steps taken together would dramatically reduce carbon emissions while helping to build a fairer world, and improve our international standing.

Chapter 24   2020 /early21 – Global crises increase amidst further deterioration in UK political standards

All the evidence confirms that global warming and species extinction are continuing at a faster pace. Reports that parts of the Amazon forest are producing CO_2, and of methane released in the arctic circle as the permafrost melts, as well as the fracturing of ice in Antarctica, indicate that feedback loops to make global warming unstoppable already exist. At the same time Covid19 is proving harder to control than first thought with widespread death, illness and the associated economic collapse.

The break in normal life caused by Covid19 gave us all time to think, learn and reassess the several crises facing us and our priorities. It has led to more and more voices calling for urgent action to curb carbon emissions.   Many have shared ideas about 'solutions' both for the climate and the economy.

This includes thousands of individual protesters, hundreds of charities and pressure groups, celebrities, as well as statutory bodies in the UK such as the Committee on Climate Change and National Infrastructure Commission and global institutions such as the World Bank, the IMF and the Pope.

Zoom meetings have blossomed to increase public knowledge of many actions, ideas and groups never mentioned in the main media. Indeed there are so many protests and zoom meetings that, even if not employed elsewhere, it is impossible to join them all. They clash.

Yet despite this, despite all the previous information from the Climate talks and the promises made in Paris, despite the declarations of an emergency by Parliament and countless local councils, the government is still pursuing 'business as usual'. It only pays lip service to supporting action against climate change.   Lip service is more dangerous than denial, because it fools people into thinking the right actions are being taken. It encourages them to 'leave it to the government'.

The Green Homes Grant is one obvious example of lip service. In the face of the need for a widespread programme of insulation and other measures to upgrade UK's poor quality housing stock, both to cut carbon emissions and improve health, the government offered a limited voucher scheme for a few months. It is complicated to access and the people trying to do so have found it difficult if not impossible to find accredited builders. The time limit was then extended due to public pressure, but the implementation was so difficult and botched that early in 2021 it was cancelled.

The Green Homes Grant follows the pattern of earlier inadequate token actions – such as solar panel payments which were hastily reduced when taken up.

It is impossible to take Boris Johnson's commitment to urgent action on the climate seriously when so many of his promises and actions are contradictory, and are almost always targets for the future. Setting targets is meaningless, often a way to delay action while appearing to wish to reform, greenwashing. Even more so as targets are frequently missed.

If the government had been serious, it would have taken all possible immediate actions to reduce carbon by cancelling major building projects, including at Heathrow; and stopped the destruction of trees and wildlife habitats caused by HS2 among other projects.

It would also have appointed someone to lead the COP talks who had a record in trying to prevent climate disaster instead of Alok Sharma, Secretary of State for Business, with a poor record on environmental issues and human rights.

Aligning climate change with business interests follows the pattern of Tory policy from the start. Margaret Thatcher is often congratulated for introducing awareness of climate change to the UK. But, significantly, she always stressed that it could only be funded by successful business. Environmental gain was an add on to business success. She offered no solution when economic action was the cause of climate change - the situation we face today. Her attitude seems to have remained the Tory position throughout.

The insignificance of climate change was confirmed by the small part it played in Johnson's conference speech. One 'green' promise - to invest £160 million in offshore wind – delivered as usual with the exaggerated language of becoming a 'world leader' in clean energy. (The easier, cheaper option of on- shore wind, was ignored.) When in contrast £24.7 billion was promised for road development; the lack of traffic in lockdown was used to fast track £200 million worth of road schemes; and Johnson promised to 'build, build, build' to restore the economy after Covid19. Concrete and steel are extremely carbon heavy.

His reassurance that technology will solve the climate crisis is the claim used by all who want to delay reform in order to continue with 'business as usual'.

The proposed new nuclear plant at Sizewell adds to the disaster. It will involve dangerous increases in carbon emissions for decades while a huge concrete building is put up before any electricity is produced. Only someone who doesn't believe in the need to cut carbon NOW could make such a proposal.

Quite apart from the known dangers of nuclear power, the unsolved problem of how to deal with the waste, its high cost, that profits will go abroad, and the fact that it is totally unnecessary. A combination of wind and tidal or wave power could supply all our needs. This country is blessed with benign sources of energy.

Many thousands of us recognised that pandemics and the environmental crises are linked, both symptoms of nature's distress. And we saw the Covid19 lockdown as a unique moment to change policies to counter all the global crises together - pandemics, climate change, pollution, species extinction as well as economic collapse, poverty, starvation and inequality - all the things killing wildlife and us and destroying civilisation.

The government is clearly in denial of these links. On the contrary, it has used Covid19 to ignore global warming and delayed related work such as reducing plastic waste. All emphasis has been on maintaining the existing carbon heavy economy and restoring it as soon as possible, with the assumption that all will go back to 'normal' once Covid19 is 'solved'. Growth of the old fashioned, carbon heavy sort ,is still the aim.

As before, the BBC news has been complicit in endorsing and repeating the government's view with almost no mention of climate change for months.

Covid19 has undoubtedly been a test of competence. The government has had to confront an unknown and very infectious virus, with no established treatments and with the added complication that many cases show no symptoms. Governments worldwide have and still are struggling with it.

The government's responses to Covid19 have revealed more about its ability, or lack of it, than any other recent policy. Because Covid19 is a life and death matter, instead of the usual vague sound bites, comments, promises and actions have been unusually closely observed and reported. The public has been given a much clearer picture. Practical details have emerged – how policy decisions actually work on the ground. As a consequence, failures have become all too obvious. Criticism from all sides has been recorded by normally supportive media and the BBC.

So how has the government performed? Dealing with Covid19 is a continuing saga but some general characteristics of the government's response are clear from the early stages. Two complete changes from their usual policies have been finding the 'money tree' and the fast progress in building hospitals and developing a vaccine using state resources. Both show that crises can be addressed quickly, that co-operation is helpful, that government needs to get involved, that expert opinion is essential, and that money can be found given political will.

However, in most other ways the government's actions have followed the ideological habits which led to the disasters of Austerity and Brexit, with no better results this time.

The 'laisse faire' attitude before the epidemic led to cuts to the NHS and to a comprehensive programme to prevent pandemics. Both of these contributed to high Covid19 deaths. When the epidemic started the government was slow and reluctant to act. Slow to take early precautions such as screening visitors from abroad, or developing testing. It seems to have been dragged into the second lockdown.

Their habit of being 'economical with the truth', so central the Leave campaign and the myth of market forces, produced the false but oft repeated claim that policy was 'following the science'.

At the start, when the WHO was urging the vital need to test, this government chose not to. Since then warnings and advice have frequently been ignored, including immediately after the first lockdown. Doctors warned opening up society would be difficult and dangerous, but Johnson and Rishi Sunak did all they could to encourage people back to the city centres, badly misjudging the dangers.

Similarly, their claim that their actions had saved the NHS from being overwhelmed was equally untrue. The NHS clearly was, and remains overwhelmed, unable to deal with routine operations or investigations. Waiting times are still growing ever longer.

Inconsistency, incoherence and incompetence have been the hallmark of their efforts. Their overall approach has changed three times. From briefly letting the virus rip to get 'herd immunity', (I wondered if this might be in the hope that all the old would die off solving the crisis in the care system); to defeating the virus as the best and only way to protect the economy; and thirdly to opposing the needs of the economy to the needs for defeating the virus, and trying to achieve 'a balance'. (Of course, to give them the benefit of the doubt, these changes may reflect learning rather than inconsistency.

Critically they have been unable to deal with the two areas that were their primary task in saving lives – PPE and test-trace-isolate. The usual pattern of exaggerated claims and targets accompanied by consistently failing performance has undoubtedly led to unnecessary deaths and a second lockdown.

Incompetence was largely the direct result of their ideological policies. Their insistence on central control, a vital plank of Tory governments since Mrs Thatcher's time, meant that local hospitals and councils were left without information. They were not involved in helping to trace contacts or produce PPE. The government's decision to take testing out of public health services also showed the same disdain for expert opinion evident when they launched the 'austerity' programme.

Their belief in market forces and their close ties and reliance on the private sector was another important factor. It led to sixteen private consultancy firms, including major companies like Deloitte, PWC, Boston Consulting Group and McKinsey being given millions of pounds worth of contracts, critically, with no evidence that they had any medical knowledge. By October 2020 the government had spent more than £2.5bn on services and equipment related to the Covid-19 pandemic, including £56m on consultancy firms.

Two companies, Serco and Deloitte, neither of which have knowledge of health issues, and both of which have been fined for failing significantly in other services, were awarded contracts for test and trace without other companies being allowed to tender for contracts. And, not surprisingly, have continued to fail. Daily reports in newspapers and by the BBC recorded widespread failure to contact people, often accompanied by yet more ambitious targets being set by the government. The whole layer of organisation needed to provide safe isolation has been largely absent.

During Covid19, the usual close contact between government and corporations, with its potential for corruption, seems to have degenerated into general malpractice. The only reason for many contracts seems to have been their links to Tory party politicians.

A special 'high priority' channel gave firms put forward by politicians a ten times greater chance of getting a contract. They were (wrongly) assumed to 'be pre-sifted for credibility'. This went. against normal practice where any links with MPs should lead to more rigorous checks because of a potential conflict of interests.

Other malpractice included issuing contracts after the work had started or been completed. Notices of some contracts were issued 5 months late. Also there were no rules as to how the high priority channel should work.

At best government procurement was grossly mismanaged, people out of touch with reality. At worst it showed the sort of corrupt 'cronyism' expected of a banana republic. The founder of the Good Law Project, Jolyon Maughan QC, called some contracts 'unlawful' (Guardian 18 November 2020) and is pursuing action.

Looking at the provision of PPE, the National Audit Office (NAO) estimated that the government paid £10 billion more than it should have on buying 5 years' worth of PPE equipment at inflated prices during the epidemic. But by the end of July, less than 10% have been delivered, some not even manufactured and, as Jolyon Maughan QC says, most will not be used. But this obscene waste of money didn't stop some care homes and hospitals being short of supplies.

The end result was a scandalous waste of money as well as failed services leading to significant numbers of unnecessary deaths. At this stage the UK had the worst record for dealing with Covid19 in Europe.

In April 2021 the whole issue of government corruption in granting contracts for Covid19 has expanded into accusations of improper relations between civil servants and businesses, and the inappropriate power of special advisers in government. (Guardian including 16 April). Lobbying by businesses will be under scrutiny, especially as the government has once again appointed an insider to oversee their report.

WHERE the government has been prepared to spend money during Covid19 is revealing. The early support for jobs in furlough which retained the status quo was understandable. But, as the longer term effects of Covid19 became more obvious (quite apart from the need to cut carbon), it should have been clear that many jobs will be unsustainable in the future and so should not be directly supported. Instead supporting all people during the crisis and investing in training for sustainable jobs would be logical and sensible.

Covid19 had also shown the value of lowly, despised and badly paid jobs. These facts, together with the Government's own policy of levelling up would suggest a generous Citizens' Income as the most effective support. But so far there has been no change in policy, despite pleas for a trial scheme from 500 parliamentarians, peers and others. It seems the government is not interested in levelling up or thinking about the jobs that will be essential in the future.

It is relevant that 'levelling up' is the usual fudge. Real 'levelling' would mean increasing low incomes but also decreasing high ones. There is no indication this is happening or planned.

A citizen's Income would save much of the money spent on maintaining the income of higher earners in furlough, as well as the cost of means testing, and would ensure that no one falls through the net. When people are unable to work by government decree, true for many during Covid19, it is essential to support them. No one should be allowed to fall through the net.

The Government was prepared to fund meals for a short time to help restaurants and pubs - Eat Out To Help Out. This expensive scheme helped some businesses but only in the short term, at the cost of £522 million. Not surprisingly it increased numbers of Covid19 infections. In contrast, at that time, the government would not fund school meals during holidays for hungry children, although it was later forced into a U-turn.

In other areas of government, while higher MPs salaries and expenses were proposed in March 2020, nurses and carers received no increase after lockdown and asylum seekers got a 3p a week increase bringing their income to £5.56 per day. The later offer of a miserable 1% increase for nurses in 2021 caused a public outcry.

Similarly, it has been prepared to pay out huge amounts on defence, including yet more Trident missiles, but has cut back on foreign aid, despite the pleas of the UN and other governments for aid to be increased to help with Covid19. It seems the government is obsessed with military status, is determined to maintain inequality in incomes and cares little for the vulnerable.

The government gained wide-ranging powers in the Covid19 emergency to enforce rules to close businesses and stop activities. Many of the people affected have accused it of abusing those powers, by making incoherent rules without giving any evidence to support them. This is a familiar aspect of our first past the post voting system, which encourages any party with a majority to push through what it likes regardless. Our voting system encourages bullying.

Other policy objectives continued during the lockdown have also been dominated by ideology. All the false promises made about Brexit – how simple it would be, how advantageous it would be - have been exposed. The long drawn out 'negotiations' which have wasted far too much money and time, have caused particular exasperation. Only weeks before the deadline no exact details were available, so businesses, farmers, the police and others didn't yet know what they have to prepare for.

The Tory party, which prides itself on being the party of business, has proved either out of touch or out of sympathy with the details of how businesses work – how long they need to make fundamental changes.

The government itself was well aware that Brexit will damage the economy and cause supply problems. It issued warning to schools about the need to stockpile. Yet it remained determined to carry Brexit through. The U-turns that have become so common in dealing with Covid19 did not apply to Brexit.

(This book will not attempt to follow the aftermath of Brexit. So far celebrating its success has been noticeably absent, and many problems have been aired – not least those in Northern Ireland. Continuing problems will probably be reported in the press, as like Covid19 they concern people's ability to survive very directly. The government may try to disguise any Brexit problems as caused by Covid19.)

The government also continued its prime objective of undermining democracy, 'shrinking the state'. The 2019 election manifesto promised to reduce the rights of parliament, as well as the power of the judiciary and people to check government actions. All essential to democracy.

The government frequently lauds democracy, and has fiercely decried those it claimed were undermining democracy, by, for example, wanting a second referendum. Yet the public should be in no doubt that this government is openly dedicated to reducing democratic control and rights.

We know that democracies can be overthrown by apparently democratic means. It has happened. We cannot say we have not been warned. Their own statements, their published manifesto have made their aims clear. Even when busy with Covid19 and Brexit, this work continued.

In July 2020 a panel selected by the Ministry of Justice started considering proposals to reduce the power of Judicial Review because they claimed it was being abused. The real reason was almost certainly because they had been defeated in the supreme court over Brexit article50 and prorogation cases and recent cases preventing deportations. In the second lockdown the government used its special power to remove the right of peaceful protest, another essential right in a functioning democracy.

The Police, Crime Sentencing and Courts Bill reached Parliament in early 2021. It is an attempt to bed these restrictions into long term law. It has led to several demonstrations, despite Covid19 restrictions and has been very widely criticised, including by two Tory MPs who warned in the Guardian that it 'may create uncertainty by giving far too much discretions to the police' and 'far too much power to the executive to change the law be decree if it chooses.'

The Home Office continues as uncaring as ever. One example reported in the Guardian, shows that nothing has been learned from the Windrush scandal. About 20 of the same staff that caused the scandal are being used to provide compensation. Complaints of racism and discrimination within the teams prompted an internal investigation and the resignation of a senior official, Alexandra Ankrah. The scheme has been described as 'systemically racist and unfit for purpose....It's not just racism. It is an unwillingness to look with any curiosity or genuine concern at the situation of victims, many of whom were elderly and unwell." A group of predominantly black and Asian people were being "re-traumatised" by the compensation scheme.

Proposals to improve the scheme were rejected. The result has been a lack of understandable information and guidance and a slow rate of compensation. By the end of October, after 18 months only £1.6m had been paid out to 196 people. This is in contrast to the thousands who were expected to apply for between £200m and £570m. At least nine people have died before receiving compensation they applied for.

Several reports indicate that racism is endemic in society, in the police force, in universities and in Government departments. Boris Johnson even broke with tradition to deny the retiring Archbishop of York a seat in the Lords, and chose Munira Mirza to head the commission on race relations, when she has disputed there is discrimination and talked instead of a 'culture of grievance'.

To add insult to injury, in early 2021 the government produced an extremely biased report, denying institutional racism and blaming those who suffer from racism or protest against it for having outdated attitudes. This divisive report has been very generally condemned including even from the heart of government.

Lord Woolley the former head of No 10's race disparity unit (Guardian 31 March 2021) said 'If you deny structural race inequality then you've got nothing to do and that in of itself is a huge problem. There was structural racism before Covid-19 and Black Lives Matter, in all areas and all levels of our society. There are shocking disparities and shocking outcomes in health, education and housing. That's why we set up the race and disparity unit in the first place'. 'Covid-19 laid bare these structural inequalities in such Technicolor and made them worse, where [BAME communities] are dying in greater numbers, becoming severely ill in greater numbers, and losing their jobs.'

'Then to be not only in denial, but saying: 'What are you complaining about? We live in a society that is much better than it was 100 years ago' is monumental disrespect and disregard of people's lived experiences, but above all a lost opportunity for systemic change'.

We cannot be surprised that the treatment of refugees and asylum seekers has also degenerated further. Priti Patel has been ramping up the 'hostile environment' by increasing the difficulties of vulnerable refugees. She has been doing all she can to stop channel crossings, including children with family connections, even suggesting illegal methods that could cause drowning. At the same time proposed changes in legislation about applying for asylum will make it much harder. It will be impossible for many traumatised victims.

The government's policies could hardly be further away from any of the reforms essential to solve global environmental and social problems. Nor do they provide a decent standard of living or even basic safety for a significant proportion of the domestic population.

Homelessness has increased since the first lockdown. Food banks are having to supply even more meals.

Mental distress has increased. We are suffering the worst recession for 300 years. Local councils responsible for much social care are being denied the funds to carry it out.

And yet another bout of 'austerity' has been promised for the future. Covid19 is a factor, and will definitely be used as the excuse, but in reality the policies of our irresponsible and uncaring government must be the major cause.

Chapter 25 What we can do. What we can we aim for.

In this bleak situation, we cannot allow the situation to remain for the next four years and more. The bad news is all too obvious. We simply cannot continue with the same policies. Even those apparently benefitting from capitalism should recognise this. Our present way of life is destroying us all.

It is completely unrealistic to hope for change through the party political system in Parliament. Our poisonous brand of party politics is a major part of the problem. Both the main parties support the status quo. They are both addicted to capitalism and fossil fuels and are both dependent on existing industries for their funding.

The Tories through their elite friends in corporations, their investments in current industries and their expectations for cushy jobs and directorships.

The Labour party, although in theory the party for 'normal' working people, has been and still is hamstrung by their links with the trades' unions and probably now too by their MPs' investments in privatisation. Their policy seems to have been to support existing jobs such as the car, nuclear and 'defence' industries, with no thought of the social and environmental costs or of potential benign alternatives.

This is really disappointing given that they have been in the perfect position to develop benign alternatives. The shop stewards' Lucas Plan of 1976 showed the way. A wonderful case of using their own expertise to design 'socially useful products' instead of armaments. Sadly, this rare example and was not accepted by the management and has not been repeated by other unions.

This book criticises Tory governments frequently, but the Labour government of Tony Blair, and their feeble, almost non-existent, behaviour in opposition are also very much to blame. They have supported capitalist growth and exploitation. They, like the Tories have insisted that work is the route to happiness, yet, like the Tories have been complacent about wages that are insufficient to live on. It is just not true to say that work pays – it doesn't pay nearly enough.

They have in effect been 'tory lite', supporting privatisation, including very expensive PPI hospitals; condoning poor wages for most and excessive bonuses for others; introducing benefits ostensibly for the poor which really subsidise industry; and, until very recently, have failed to give climate change any consideration.

They, like the Tories have supported wars of intervention which have destroyed other countries and destabilised the world. And the horror and incredible expense of nuclear weapons.

Before becoming a member of the Green Party I used to vote Labour. I even voted for Tony Blair, but told him I never would again after the Iraq war. I think the treatment Jeremy Corbyn's more ethical policies and his stance against nuclear weapons got, tells us all we need to know about the morals of the current Labour Party. The current suppression of debate within the party is sinister. It adds to our problems, as does Sir Kier Starmer's view of 'patriotism'.

My view of patriotism is the opposite. Patriotism involves a love of one's land and all the natural life it sustains (including people) and a pride in the country's ethical policies. Anyone proud of the UK as it is is in deep denial. True patriots now are the whistleblowers who warn of real dangers and those who try to protect our natural systems or the quality of people's lives, whether in small ways or large. People who expect high standards and are doing all they can to bring them about.

This includes people as varied as Isabella Tree who with her husband has worked for years to restore wildlife on their farm (which they could not have done without the support of the EU), hosts of smaller organic gardeners and farmers and those promoting grow your own during lockdown, to those, like Shelter, who campaign for decent housing to those who provide food banks.

It should be clear that the good in this country comes from myriad people and often happens despite government not because of government.   It is also important to recognise that loving one's own land and being proud of it in no way should lead anyone to put others' love of their lands down. Patriotism is not jingoism.

The Green Party has all along seen the essential connection between a healthy environment and social justice. It has had plenty of policies to offer on every issue but has had no power. Ironically, it has been able to develop realistic policies precisely because of its independence from big pressure groups. Left alone it has been able to think things through from first principles.

But the resulting lack of finance has been a major factor in reducing its impact. Sadly, its aim to gain power from the grass roots by building on local government gains will be far too slow in the present emergency. From this we should learn that in future money should not be allowed to buy elections. The election process and political party expenses needs to be carefully controlled to produce a level playing field in which all views are easily accessible.

Our present system would allow the Tories with their large unrepresentative majority, to hang on for four more years of increasingly damaging policies. From their past performance and stated aims we can predict that the Tory party, now dominated by UKIP philosophy, will fail to give priority to the pressing environmental and social crises; will continue a devastating aggressive foreign policy and will hamper protest by weakening and dismantling democratic power and institutions here.   The Labour party seems reconciled to this timetable and is largely in denial about their poor prospects of ever getting to power, even if they manage to stop infighting.

Even at this moment of crises, the two main political parties have remained straight-jacketed in their out dated, divisive habits. Like bankers they exist in a parallel world which has nothing to do with real threats or opportunities. They do not attend to the real concerns of the public. And certainly will not respond with the speed needed for the current emergencies. Failing to recognise that Covid19 is intimately linked, and a symptom of, the climate change and species extinction is central to the problem and causing yet more delay.

Even if enough conscience stricken Tory MPs resigned or crossed the floor to bring the government down, a general election on its own would bring no advantage.

My hope comes entirely from the other side of the equation – civil society - the public, particularly the young, many of whom seem better informed than their elders. Covid19 has brought about a transformation in public attitudes. It has brought us closer together. It has shown that people of all sorts can work together to help each other and are stronger for working together. Colour, age, religion, political loyalties are as nothing in the face of life and humanity. It has shown the importance of local communities. It has made new heroes. And it has shown how much people value nature and want to protect it.

If there is a silver lining to Covid19, it rests on this new found grass roots energy and sympathy and on two other facts. First, that our vulnerability has been exposed. For the first time many have started to worry about the prospect of global famine or water shortages. We have realised just how vulnerable sophisticated western societies are to any small change in circumstances. How all the necessities of life – clean water, food, heating, communications – rely on just-in-time deliveries from long supply chains, correctly functioning complicated systems and a healthy workforce.

We are the very opposite of self-sufficient. In many ways more vulnerable than poorer people who grow their own food and fetch their water. The difficulties in shopping and the loss of jobs have shown that our present way of life is uncertain, and that change can come extremely quickly – out of the blue. This, I hope will give urgency, a greater sympathy for others, and the wish to work together to solve imminent common problems to survive.

Second, our present system of government has been proved criminally negligent, weak and incapable of keeping us safe. Although it has been dragged into several U-turns over Covid19, we are nowhere near persuading it to introduce effective reforms. There is no evidence that it has appreciated the emergency of climate breakdown. It would be taking immediate action if it had. All we are being offered is green-washing; an exercise in delaying change, or skewing it to the advantage of existing industries. A matter of placating the public while continuing to profit from the status quo.

However, from these small changes, the many U-turns, we know that when a wide alliance come together and insist, with the help of social media, they have an effect. We have gained confidence. The bigger changes needed so urgently are possible if we are prepared to act.

The media has played its part. Covid19 has proved too important for the media to gloss over mistakes in its usual unconditional support for government. They have been driven to look at the facts and expose mistakes. Brexit should lead to the same informed reporting as this too will affect many people's livelihoods. And Brexit cannot be excused as an unexpected global disaster that all governments are having to cope with. It was a deliberate choice of policy, with years to develop all aspects of the repercussions – definitely an own goal.

Unfortunately, there is no evidence the media are any more realistic about climate breakdown.

So, now it is all down to us! Greta Thunberg has said 'the real power is with the people'. She is right, but, obviously, only if we take it. In the past in the UK most people have been very reluctant to act, leaving protest to the few or trusting the government. For many the situation does not seem to have been bad enough to prompt action. And those really suffering have probably been so fully engaged in personal survival they have not been in a position to do more.

But at this time of undeniable crises which will overwhelm all of us and steal our children's futures, those of us who can would be irresponsible not to join together and act in far greater numbers. Getting in touch is easy for most of us – but not all - with social media. Plenty of people are well practised in it already.

It is everyone's democratic duty to oust a government that is undermining safety and democracy. It is immoral to leave it to a few thousand willing to break the law and pay the personal price. And, anyway, we know that hasn't worked. In a democracy the government can only rule with the consent of the people.

The government can do, and has done, its best to tie our hands with all sorts of institutional hurdles. But unlike a dictatorship, they are not likely to mow us down in the streets. We will not have to face the dangers many people already suffer in other countries. For this reason we are uniquely able to act.

In the final analysis, the quality of any democracy has always depended on the public - to understand the predicaments and choose wise leaders, or reject them. At this moment of crises, when our survival depends on drastic reform, we can no longer condone dangerous policies that go against the advice of the UN, the government's own targets and agreements, the advice from countless of our own institutions as well as our own personal moral convictions. A government that frequently breaks the law and its own standards. It has been exposed as a rogue government. We need to withhold our consent or we will be complicit in our own downfall and the tragedies our policies are causing abroad.

Only those of us alive now can enforce the essential reforms to save ourselves and future generations. We are not angels, but at least most of us are much more in touch with reality and value and show kindness and intelligence in the way we lead our lives. We are not excessively greedy or blinded by delusions of power.

Together we need to make it crystal clear, particularly to those of the public not yet engaged, that we do not approve current policies. MPs always claim the public supports their actions. I don't. None of my friends do, but maybe a significant number of the public still think the government knows best. So, one of our very first tasks is to set the record straight – to explain loud and clear to the public how policies are based on false myths that have patently failed

We must challenge the lies and stereotypes. There is no alternative to detailed conversations picking myths and facts apart. We then have to rely on people's ability to recognise the truth.

Even those who don't care about fairness and lack sympathy for others, including their own children, should realise that the rapid pace of change threatens their own lives (except maybe for the very old.) Climate change is here. It has been having drastic effects in many countries already and we will soon suffer more effects in the UK.

We must also learn from the mistakes of past campaigns. A very basic mistake among campaigners was the assumption that if we showed how important an issue was by paying a personal cost - going to prison or paying fines - governments would be impressed and respond. Other people would be impressed and join in. The task was one of explaining the situation. Sadly, this was a fallacy. For most people the personal cost was too high. And, as for governments, an articulate student recently stressed in a zoom meeting that 'the government knows, it just doesn't care'.

Extinction Rebellion's use of 'swarming', a way of stopping traffic without getting arrested, which allowed many more to join in was a step in the right direction. Their first actions were impressive in highlighting the environmental disasters. However, the Achille's heel of their work is that it relies on a treacherous media. Only actions leading to arrests are of any interest to the media, so protesters were back to square one, having to pay a personal price. And that automatically limited who can get involved, quite apart from the media's interest in misrepresenting their aims. Covid19, too, has made such actions very difficult.

Another mistake in the past has been 'competition', even 'tribalism', between protesters. Protesters who shared the same aim have often not co-operated with each other. I found it hard to understand why CND, for example, did not support PICAT, the court action against Trident. It was designed to be easy to carry out, with no personal costs. I managed it when in relatively poor health. All it needed was phone calls, emails and signatures. It was a gift to CND and other peace movements. Who can tell whether, had they joined in to produce thousands of signatures rather than hundreds, the press might have publicised it and the Attorney General might have been pressured to allow court hearings?

Similarly, some Extinction Rebellion members seem to disdain other types of protest, assuming only their methods will work. We need to recognise that we are usually working at different bits of the same problem. Environmental justice goes hand in hand with social justice.

So we need to support each other in a range of protests which do not inflict a high personal cost, although inevitably they will involve work.

More important we must come together to agree a common vision for society. We are the many. The total membership of the countless groups working for the interlinked issues of peace, social justice, care of wildlife and the environment, for democratic and economic reform and for sustainable living must be truly enormous. This includes not only protest groups such as Greenpeace, Friends of the Earth, Eradicating Ecocide, Shelter, CND, CAAT, Occupy, anti-fracking groups, Amnesty, Black Lives Matter, Hope not Hate, Fridayforfuture, Me too, Extinction Rebellion, etc, but also countless very varied community projects such as the Transition Towns, community energy groups, food banks, wildlife conservation groups, allotment associations.

My impression during lockdown was of a staggering amount of grass roots activity quite independent of government and ignored by the media. An unrecognised groundswell of knowledge and action. Most if not all of these people are not at all happy with the status quo. If we add the 48% who voted Remain, and others who will find Brexit harms their way of life, we almost certainly have a clear majority in the country.

If we share information, learn from each other, support each other and agree a common demand, it must succeed.

One simple way to augment the impact of a any demonstration is for all those who cannot attend to email their support. I am surprised this has not happened already. So far, my requests for ways to do this, as my health has stopped me participating on the ground, have gone unanswered.

All types of protest are equally valid, from strikes to lobbying, demonstrations, disturbance and the law. Extinction Rebellion is against violence. I agree with them, not because it doesn't work but

169

because the destruction and trauma bring a train of terrible consequences which often last for a long time. Also violence can quickly get out of hand. The ends do not justify the means. The means dictate the ends.

There is a clear line between disturbance and damage to property, such as breaking windows, and violence to people. Our laws accept that it is legal to damage in order to prevent a greater damage. To break down a door, for example, to put out a fire.

This defence has been successfully used in many trials, including in 1996 by two women charged with causing £1.5m damage to a Hawk fighter jet. They did this to prevent its use in the bombing of East Timor by Indonesia, which would have broken international law.

The same defence was used in 2001 by two anti-nuclear protesters charged with conspiracy to cause criminal damage to a Trident submarine in a Barrow-in-Furness shipyard.   Violence in self-defence is also legal. If milder forms of protests and lobbying are ignored, damage and disturbance have to follow.

So, the dual purpose of campaigning must be to influence and engage more of the public and to make life so difficult for the government that they choose to consider changes.

But this will not be enough. When the daily figures on CO_2 levels in the atmosphere are 420 and more, but these are not headline news every day. And when countless experts tell us we must act NOW, but the conversations in the press and government are set in years to come, we are in real trouble. We are failing.

We must learn from this and fast. Campaigning alone will not work. Asking the government to make changes cannot work. It is blindingly obvious that the government is simply incapable of organising or instituting real change. If we continue to just petition and lobby them– we are choosing to fail.

Right now, Civil Society needs to take matters into its own hands. The large scale system changes we want need to be planned and clearly expressed. Demanding change without being explicit is a recipe for disaster. Moments of change are tricky. They can easily go wrong. There needs to be a clear and agreed vision for the future to give all of us an understanding of the need to change and the many positive gains to come from sustainable living.

I agree with many others that, as in war, we need a Government of National Unity. It has happened. It is possible and can happen quickly.

I also agree with Extinction Rebellion that, reform must come from the grass roots. Since politicians have failed so badly, the National Government must be directed by Citizens' Assemblies. It is difficult to image some leading Tories being able to co-operate with others on a very different programme and one dictated by Citizen's Assemblies. Perhaps keeping their seats and their pay will prove persuasive.

So, another immediate task, in addition to campaigning, is to initiate Citizens' Assemblies. To build a parallel, complimentary system for national government using assemblies and referenda. We cannot wait any longer. We cannot wait to be disappointed by the upcoming COP talks. The world cannot wait. All those islands threatened by sea level rise cannot wait. The desperate people of Yemen cannot wait. It would be criminally negligent to wait.

The task will fall to any concerned members of the public, but mostly to the great and the good, the many institutions that have been calling for action. It sounds daunting. It would be totally overwhelming if the answers were not all there already. There is plenty of expertise about environmental, social and economic needs and potential solutions across the country. In universities and other bodies including charities and pressure groups and in countless work places. Many experts will probably continue to share their knowledge freely, but crowd funding may be required for meetings and reports. That is another way for the public to demonstrate their support. Expert opinion will need to be scrutinised and agreed by Citizen's Assemblies. We know enough about top down solutions and the risk of eccentric so called experts not to trust them implicitly.

The need for reform is immense and covers almost every policy area. It will take time. However, in the immediate future, a limited list of top priorities should be developed by Citizens' Assemblies and announced as the Manifesto for a National Government of Unity.

In this way a Manifesto can be produced within weeks or months – certainly before COP. Whether one Citizens' Assembly should consider each topic or whether several smaller ones across the country should be involved is something to be decided.

I suggest this manifesto should promise immediate action to avert both the social and environmental crises. A generous Citizens' Income to support everyone through the changes and swift action to curb the environmental crises by a moratorium on all carbon heavy infrastructure projects, and those threatening wildlife as well as introducing a carbon tax.

It should promise to restore the services destroyed by austerity and privatisation and to reform our foreign and misnamed defence policy as a matter of urgency to help restore global peace and save money for useful purposes.

It should promise training for all whose jobs will no longer be sustainable, as well as a comprehensive overhaul of tax and economic policies. We no longer want to be known for tax havens and money laundering.

All changes will be stipulated by Citizens' Assemblies and may be confirmed by referenda. Before the end of the parliament it should promise to reform our voting system, and develop a constitution suited to today's needs. I hope this will include means by which voters can get rid of unsatisfactory MPs more easily and quickly.

An important feature of the new constitution should be the principle of subsidiarity – that is making decisions as locally as possible. Giving responsibility and power to local councils for local services and policies would transform government in this country. It would encourage many more talented people to get involved, and provide much more information. I think it might have big implications for Scotland and Wales.

I also hope the Citizens' Assemblies will endorse the other principles outlined in this book for global reform. (I suspect Citizens' Assemblies will be needed at the global level to counter the unrepresentative control of banks and global institutions. People in the Third World will have an important part to play.)

As soon as possible, national and regional citizens assemblies should be set up to educate ourselves about the whole range of policies; to develop a more detailed vision of the kind of society we want to live in; and to play our role in government.

Citizen's Assemblies should become part of a grass roots participatory democracy. Perhaps universities and colleges could help organise these. It will be a huge task in our complicated, sophisticated world. But It will be transformative process. Knowledge brings power. Informed people can no longer be easily fooled by lies and slogans. We should become the informed and active public that is an essential for a functioning democracy.

The aim remains to return to party political rule as soon as is practical with Citizens' Assemblies continuing in their role. In this Anthropocene age they should form part of any government in the future. Only in this way, by a participatory democracy, engaging people at all levels of government and in all walks of life, can governments hope to have enough information to deal with the speed of change and the complexities of our sophisticated world, where man's actions are a controlling force.

None of this should stop us from doing other positive things ourselves. Many people and groups are doing just that already. In a recent zoom meeting, Bill Dunster of Zed Power and Agememmnon Otero from Repowering London and Energy Gardens described several small scale sustainable projects, and showed how simple and cheap the technology is. They stressed that DIY projects are possible for 'normal' people even under present conditions. You do not need complicated grants and professional builders. Other zoom meetings testify to a multitude of enthusiastic local initiatives improving life and the environment in different ways.

The UK is full of good, enthusiastic and ingenious people. We need large scale system change, but meanwhile small scale initiatives are a great help. They can only help to promote system change by making people realise their own power.

All of us can choose to live more sustainably and shop wisely, using our consumer power to encourage sustainable products and processes. It is not easy and often involves weighing up disadvantages. For example, avoiding dairy foods may mean buying GM soya milk, or almond milk intensively grown in California, which recent reports have shown is killing bees there.

Eleven factors to consider were listed after a local meeting in 2019 to encourage sustainable shopping. These included the carbon footprint of the shops involved, delivery, processes used, packaging and any pollution; the living standards/ wages of workers involved; the danger to wildlife – eg orangutans from palm oil production; support for the local economy; and fair tax.

The recommendations were to use local shops, markets and charity shops for food and other small items; similarly, to use locally owned cafes and restaurants; to eat as much unprocessed, local seasonal fresh food as possible; to cut down on meat and fish; to eat organic where possible. Only organic foods are sure not to have used pesticides, oil based fertiliser on plants, medicines and hormones on meat, or additives to increase bulk, improve taste and shelf life.

We should also use our votes wisely at council or byelections, or, even better, consider standing ourselves.